Introduction

Welcome to the Science Doctor KS3 physics workbook.

This book covers the majority of the physics in the Key Stage 3 national curriculum and is designed to be completed independently by students between the ages of 11 and 14.

Students should first of all carefully read the notes on each topic. They should then use their comprehension skills and scientific knowledge to answer the questions.

Once completed, students can check their answers with those at the back. I'd recommend correcting any incorrect answers in a different coloured pen.

I hope you find the book useful, and good luck in your physics studies!

Dr Peter Edmunds

Dedicated to my wife Helen (who definitely didn't make me write this), our cats Buddy, Henry & Herbert and a tiny human who I've not yet had the pleasure of meeting.

Special thanks are also reserved for William Barron de Burgh and my father Professor David Edmunds for their work in proofreading this book.

Contents

Tick each ☐ once the topic is completed.

Energy

Energy stores

Energy is not a physical thing that we can see or touch.

Different objects **store** energy in different ways. These are called **energy stores** and are listed below:

Name	Description	Examples
Thermal	Any object with a **temperature** has a thermal energy store. The higher the temperature of an object, the more energy in the thermal energy store.	A hot cup of tea, hot bath water, a hot radiator.
Kinetic	Any object that is **moving** has a kinetic energy store. The faster the movement, the more energy in the kinetic energy store.	A car or train that is moving, somebody walking or running.
Gravitational potential	Objects at a **height above the ground** have a gravitational potential energy store. The larger the height above the ground, the more energy in the gravitational potential energy store.	A book on a high shelf, a bird standing on a high branch of a tree.
Elastic potential	When objects such as a spring or elastic band are **stretched** or **compressed** they store elastic potential energy. The greater the extension or compression, the larger the elastic potential energy store.	A stretched elastic band/spring/hair tie.
Chemical	Different **chemicals** store energy in their chemical energy store.	Food, fuel, batteries.
Nuclear	Energy that is stored in the **nucleus** of an atom is in the nuclear energy store.	Fuel in nuclear power plants. For example, uranium or plutonium.
Magnetic potential	When two **magnets** are held close together, they have a magnetic potential energy store.	Two magnets near each other.
Electrostatic potential	When **charges** are close together, they have an electric potential energy store.	Protons, electrons, any charged particle.

Q1. A helicopter is stationary and hovering above the ground. State the energy store the helicopter has.

....

Q2. The helicopter now starts to move forwards. State another energy store the helicopter now has.

....

Q3. While flying, the engine of the helicopter becomes warm. State the energy store the engine of the helicopter has.

....

Q4. The helicopter uses a fuel called kerosene (similar to petrol). State the energy store that kerosene has.

....

Q5. Somebody is bungee jumping and jumps off a bridge. State what happens to their gravitational potential energy store as they fall.

....

Q6. As the person bungee jumps, they accelerate and get faster. State what happens to their kinetic energy store.

....

Q7. When the person gets to the bottom of their bungee jump, the bungee cord stretches. State what happens to its elastic potential energy store.

....

Q8. A remote-controlled car has a battery that powers it. State the energy store the battery has.

....

Q9. The remote-controlled car accelerates forwards. State the energy store that it now has.

....

Q10. The battery of the remote-controlled car becomes hot as it is being used. State which energy store has increased.

....

Q11. State the energy store that two charged particles close to each other have.

....

Q12. State the energy store that uranium fuel in a nuclear power plant has.

....

Q13. State the energy store that a chocolate bar has.

....

Q14. State the energy store that two magnets near each other have.

....

Energy transfers

The **principle of conservation of energy** tells us that energy is never created or destroyed; it is only transferred from one energy store to another.

The unit of energy is the **Joule (J)**.

There are four **pathways** for energy to be transferred from one store to another. Energy can be transferred:

1. **Mechanically.** Mechanical work is done on an object when a force is applied over a distance.
2. **Electrically.** Electrical work is done when charges move through a circuit.
3. By **heating.** The transfer of energy from a hotter object to a cooler object.
4. By **radiation.** This includes energy transferred by light (or any electromagnetic wave) and sound.

Note the phrase "work" has been used in some of the pathways. "Work done" is just another way of saying energy transferred from one store to another.

The diagram to the right shows a pendulum swinging from side to side.

In position 1, the pendulum is at its maximum height and it has a gravitational potential energy (GPE) store of 10 J.

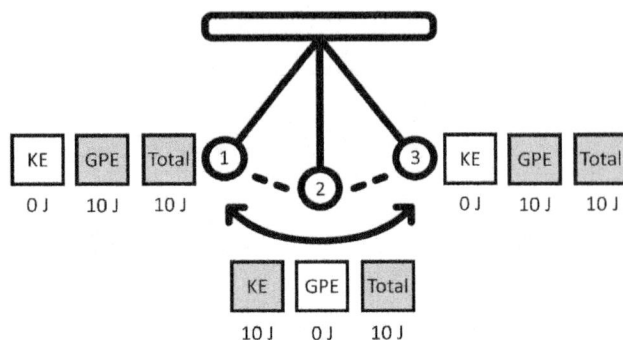

KE	GPE	Total
0 J	10 J	10 J

KE	GPE	Total
0 J	10 J	10 J

KE	GPE	Total
10 J	0 J	10 J

As the pendulum falls into position 2, gravity does mechanical work on the pendulum. The pendulum speeds up and becomes lower in height. Its GPE store empties, and its kinetic energy (KE) store fills to 10 J. Note how the overall amount of energy is the same, due to the principle of conservation of energy.

The pendulum then continues swinging to position 3. As it does so, its KE store empties and its GPE store fills back to the original 10 J. The pendulum is stationary at position 3 so it has no KE. It is also at its maximum height, so it has maximum GPE. The total energy is still unchanged.

However, the pendulum will eventually come to a stop. This is primarily due to air resistance. Generally, energy transfers are not 100% **efficient**. Energy is "wasted" by raising the thermal energy store of the surroundings. The temperature of the pendulum and the nearby air will be raised slightly.

Q1. State the principle of conservation of energy.

....

....

Q2. Describe what it means when we say that work is done on an object.

....

....

Q3. State the unit of energy.

....

Q4. A book is on a shelf and has an initial gravitational potential energy store of 30 J. It then falls off the shelf. State how much energy is in the kinetic energy store by the time the book reaches the ground.

....

Q5. In practice, the amount of energy in the kinetic energy store will be less than your answer to Q4. Describe why.

....

....

Q6. State the four pathways for energy transfer.

....

Q7. The diagram below shows the different energy stores involved in firing an arrow from a bow. Before the arrow is released, there is 20 J of energy in the elastic potential energy (EPE) store. Complete the missing energies after the arrow has been fired.

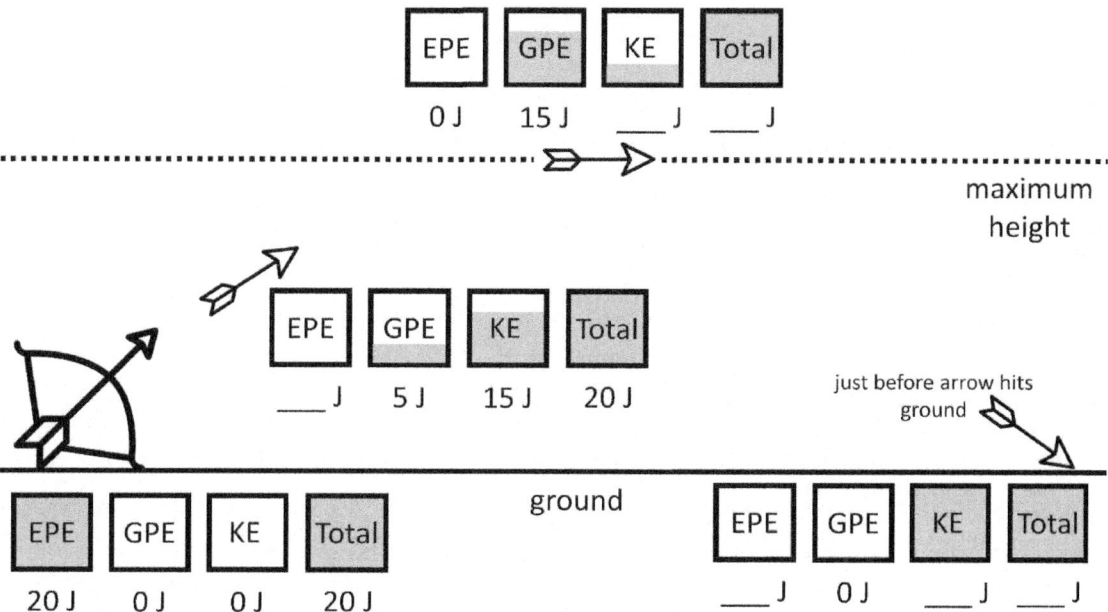

| EPE | GPE | KE | Total |
| 0 J | 15 J | ___ J | ___ J |

maximum height

| EPE | GPE | KE | Total |
| ___ J | 5 J | 15 J | 20 J |

just before arrow hits ground

ground

| EPE | GPE | KE | Total |
| 20 J | 0 J | 0 J | 20 J |

| EPE | GPE | KE | Total |
| ___ J | 0 J | ___ J | ___ J |

Power

Power is defined as the rate at which energy is transferred. The unit of power is the **Watt (W)**.

There is an equation that relates power, energy and time:

$$\text{Power} = \text{Energy} \div \text{Time} \quad \text{or in symbols} \quad P = E \div t$$

Remember, the unit of energy is the Joule (J) and the unit of time is the second (s).

We can also rearrange this equation to give:

$$\text{Energy} = \text{Power} \times \text{Time} \quad \text{or in symbols} \quad E = P \times t$$

Example question 1:

A torch has a power of 5 W and is used for a time of 30 s. Calculate the energy used by the torch.

Step 1. Write down equation:	$E = P \times t$
Step 2. Insert variables into equation:	$= 5 \times 30$
Step 3. Calculate answer. Remember units:	$= 150$ J

Example question 2:

A toaster uses 20 000 J of energy in a time of 100 s. Calculate the power of the toaster.

Step 1. Write down equation:	$P = E \div t$
Step 2. Insert variables into equation:	$= 20\,000 \div 100$
Step 3. Calculate answer. Remember units:	$= 200$ W

Sometimes power is given in units of **kilowatts (kW)**. One kilowatt is equal to one thousand watts.

To convert from kilowatts to watts you need to multiply the number of kilowatts by one thousand: **kW × 1000 → W**

To convert from watts to kilowatts you need to divide the number of watts by one thousand: **W ÷ 1000 → kW**

Q1. State the equation that links power, energy and time.

....

Q2. State the unit of power.

.............**J**...

Q3. A lamp uses an energy of 2400 J in a time of 40 s. Calculate the power of the lamp

$$P = E \div t$$

$$= 2400\ J \div 40\ s$$

= _____ W

Q4. The electric motor in a radio controlled car uses an energy of 4000 J in a time of 200 s. Calculate the power of the electric motor.

___ = ___ ÷ ___

= _____ __ ÷ _____ __

= _____ __

Q5. A microwave has a power of 900 W. Calculate how much energy it will use in a time of 15 s.

$$E = P \times t$$

= _____ __ × _____ __

= _____ J

Q6. An electric radiator has a power of 2000 W. Calculate how much energy it will use in a time of 90 s.

___ = ___ × ___

= _____ __ × _____ __

= _____ __

Q7. State how many watts are in one kilowatt.

....

Q8. Practise converting between watts and kilowatts by filling in each of the blank powers below.

| 5 kW | 1.5 kW | 2000 W | 800 W | 0.2 kW |
| = _____ W | = _____ W | = _____ kW | = _____ kW | = _____ W |

Q9. A washing machine has a power of 2.2 kW. Calculate how much energy it uses in 20 minutes. You will need to convert kilowatts into watts and minutes into seconds.

....

....

Energy resources

We generate electricity through two categories of energy resource: those that are **non-renewable** and those that are **renewable**.

A non-renewable resource is one which cannot be replaced once it has been used. One day, non-renewable resources will run out.

The most common non-renewable resources are the three **fossil fuels** (oil, coal and gas) and **nuclear power**.

As well as being used in power plants, fossil fuels can be used for **transport** and **heating**. For example, petrol and diesel (which are both made from oil) are used in cars. Gas is commonly used in central heating systems, and coal is burnt in some fireplaces.

The main advantage of using a non-renewable resource in a power plant is that they all produce a **reliable** output.

However, the main disadvantage is that burning fossil fuels increases the amount of carbon dioxide (CO_2) in the atmosphere. Carbon dioxide is a **greenhouse gas**. Greenhouse gases are responsible for **global warming** (a raising of the average temperature of Earth).

Burning coal and oil also produces **sulfur dioxide** which contributes to **acid rain**.

Nuclear power plants do not have carbon dioxide or sulfur dioxide emissions but they do produce **radioactive waste** which is difficult to dispose of safely. However, they do generate a reliable and large output.

A **renewable** resource will not run out. Three renewable resources are listed below:

Resource	Advantage	Disadvantage
Wind	No carbon dioxide emissions, so they do not contribute to global warming.	It is not always windy, so the output is unreliable. Noisy & spoils the view.
Hydro-electric		Requires the flooding of a valley with a dam. This causes a loss of habitat.
Solar	Once built, no fuel costs and so are cheap to run.	Only work in direct sunlight, so do not generate electricity at night.

We are using more renewable resources for generating electricity. In 2022, there was an "energy crisis" due to shortages of oil and gas. This shortage increased the price of electricity. Renewable resources can help reduce our reliance on fossil fuels.

Q1. Describe what a non-renewable resource is.

....

....

Q2. State the three fossil fuels.

....

Q3. Describe what a renewable resource is.

....

....

Q4. State three renewable resources.

....

Q5. The following statements are either true or false. State which are true and which are false.

    a) Nuclear power is a renewable resource.

....

    b) Wind power has an unreliable output.

....

    c) Solar power generates electricity at night.

....

Q6. Describe one disadvantage of burning fossil fuels.

....

....

Q7. Other than their use in power plants, state two uses of fossil fuels.

....

Q8. Describe general advantages of using renewable energy resources.

....

....

Q9. Hydroelectric power involves storing water at a height behind a dam. The water is then allowed to fall. State the initial energy store the water has, and the store it is transferred to as it falls.

....

Q10. State which fossil fuels produce sulfur dioxide emissions. Include what sulfur dioxide emissions lead to.

....

Q11. State the advantage of burning fossil fuels in a power plant.

....

Electricity bills

We've already learnt, on page 8, that one unit of energy is the **Joule (J)**. Two other units of energy are:

1. The **kilojoule (kJ)**. One kilojoule is equal to one thousand joules.
2. The **kilowatt hour (kWh)**. One kilowatt hour is equivalent to an electrical device with a power of 1 kW (equal to 1000 W) being used for a time of one hour. As there are 3600 seconds in one hour, one kilowatt hour is therefore equal to 3 600 000 J of energy.

We use kilowatt hours for electricity bills. This is because electrical devices in the average UK household transfer over 10 billion joules of energy a year. It's more convenient to use kilowatt hours as this brings the numbers down to a more manageable size.

Electrical devices in the average UK household transfer 3000 kWh of energy each year.

To calculate the amount of energy in kWh that a device transfers you need to multiply the power of the device (in kW) by the time that it is used for (in hours):

Energy (in kWh) = Power (in kW) × time used (in h)

As of April 2022, the price for each kWh in the UK was 28 p. To calculate the cost of an electricity bill we use the equation:

Total cost (in pence) = Energy transferred (in kWh) × price per kWh (in pence)

Example question:

Using the meter readings to the right, calculate the cost of the monthly electricity bill. The price of each kWh is 28 p.

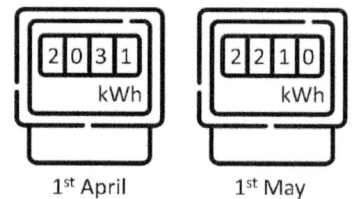

| 2 | 0 | 3 | 1 |
kWh
1st April

| 2 | 2 | 1 | 0 |
kWh
1st May

Step 1. Calculate the total number of kWh used.

To do this, we need to look at the difference in meter readings:

2210 − 2031 = 179 kWh

Step 2. Calculate cost by multiplying total number of kWh by cost per kWh.

179 × 28 = 5012 p

There are 100 p in a pound. To convert from pence to pounds you need to divide the number of pence by one hundred: **p ÷ 100 → £**

In other words, the 5012 p we calculated is equal to £50.12.

Q1. State how many joules are in a kilojoule.

....

Q2. State how many seconds are in an hour.

....

Q3. State how many joules are in a kilowatt hour.

....

Q4. An electric oven has a power of 2.2 kW and is used for a time of one hour. Calculate how much energy is used in kWh.

....

....

Q5. A television has a power of 0.2 kW and is used for a time of 8 hours. Calculate how much energy is used in kWh.

....

....

Q6. A hairdryer has a power of 1.8 kW and is used for a time of 30 minutes. Calculate how much energy is used in kWh.

....

....

Q7. State the equation that we can use to calculate cost of an electricity bill.

....

Q8. Using the meter readings to the right, calculate the cost (in pence) of the monthly electricity bill. The price of each kWh is 30 p.

 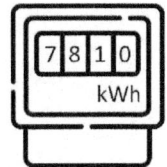

1st November   1st December

....

....

....

 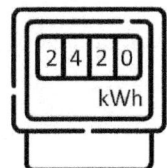

1st June   1st July

Q9. Using the meter readings to the left, calculate the cost (in pence) of the monthly electricity bill. The price of each kWh is 25 p.

....

....

....

Q10. Using the meter readings to the right, calculate the cost (in pounds) of the monthly electricity bill. The price of each kWh is 28p.

1st March   1st April

....

....

....

Thermal energy transfer

There are three ways that thermal energy can be transferred:

1. **Conduction**.
2. **Convection**.
3. **Radiation**.

Thermal energy is transferred from hotter objects to colder objects.

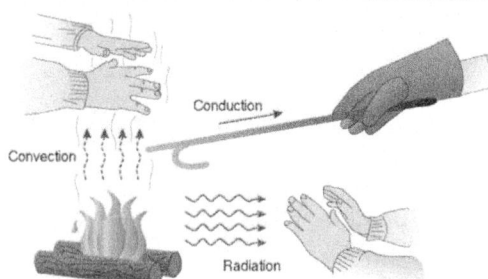

Kmecfiunit, cmglee CC BY-SA 4.0, via Wikimedia Commons

Conduction occurs primarily in solids. As particles in a solid are heated, they vibrate more. These vibrations cause collisions between particles and the vibrations are transferred along the material.

If a material is able to conduct heat well, it is called a **conductor**. Metals are one example of a good conductor.

If a material is not able to conduct heat well, it is called an **insulator**. Plastics are an example of a good insulator. Gases (like air) are very good insulators, as their particles are far apart from each other.

There are no particles in a vacuum. Conduction is not possible through a vacuum.

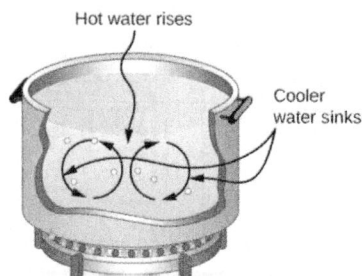

OpenStax College. *Located at:* openstax.org/books/college-physics/pages/14-6-convection *License:* CC BY: Attribution.

Convection happens in both liquids and gases. As a liquid or gas is heated, the particles move faster and become more spread out. Due to this they become less dense and therefore rise. Colder liquids or gases are more dense and sink. This is a **convection current**.

This is shown in the image on the left with a pan on a gas stove. The bottom of the pan is hot and so water at the bottom of the pan heats up and rises. Meanwhile, water at the top of the pan cools and sinks.

All objects emit **radiation** in the form of infrared waves. This can be referred to as thermal radiation or infrared radiation. As infrared radiation is an electromagnetic wave, it can even travel through a vacuum. This is how thermal radiation reaches the Earth from the Sun.

Matt black objects absorb the most infrared radiation, while shiny silver surfaces reflect infrared radiation.

Q1. State three ways thermal energy can be transferred.

Q2. The following statements are either true or false. State which are true and which are false.

a) Conduction happens mostly in solids.

b) Metals are good conductors.

c) Convection currents happen only in liquids.

d) Thermal energy cannot be transferred through a vacuum.

e) Only hot objects emit infrared radiation.

f) Thermal energy is transferred from hotter objects to colder objects.

Q3. Describe why gases are good insulators.

Q4. Describe how a convection current forms.

Q5. Describe how conduction transfers thermal energy.

Q6. State which colour of object absorbs infrared radiation the best.

Q7. Describe what a vacuum is.

Q8. Describe what a conductor is.

Q9. State which type of thermal energy transfer allows the Earth to be heated by the Sun.

Reducing unwanted thermal energy transfers

To reduce the size of electricity and fuel bills, it is important to reduce thermal energy losses from a home:

More thermal energy escaping from home ➡ More energy/fuel needed ➡ Higher heating costs

In the average home:

- 35% of thermal energy loss is through the walls. This can be reduced with **cavity wall insulation**. A cavity wall is made of two separate walls with a gap in between them. This gap can then be filled with an insulator. This is shown in the diagram to the right.
- 25% of thermal energy loss is through the roof/attic. This can be reduced with **loft insulation**.
- 25% of thermal energy loss is through windows and doors. This can be reduced with **double glazing, closing the curtains** and with a **draught excluder** that stop draughts coming in through the bottom of the door.
- 15% of thermal energy loss is through the floor. This can be reduced by improving the insulation in the floor.

Mok9, Public domain, via Wikimedia Commons

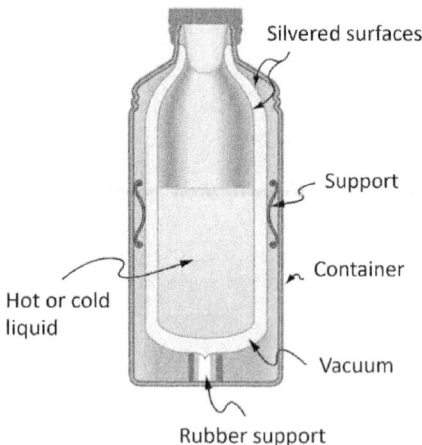

Silvered surfaces

Support

Container

Hot or cold liquid

Vacuum

Rubber support

OpenStax College. Located at: openstax.org/books/college-physics/pages/14-conceptual-questions License: CC BY: Attribution.

Vacuum flasks are also designed to limit thermal energy transfers. If a hot liquid is inside a vacuum flask, the following features keep the liquid hot for as long as possible:

- The **silvered surfaces** reflect infrared radiation back into the liquid.
- The **vacuum** does not allow for conduction or convection as there are no particles.
- The plastic lid is an **insulator**, limiting conduction. It also prevents evaporation of liquid.

They also work keep a cold liquid cooler for longer. The silvered surfaces now reflect infrared radiation away from the liquid. The vacuum prevents conduction and convection and the plastic lid also limits conduction.

Q1. State how thermal energy loss can be reduced through the:

    a) Walls of a house.

....

    b) Roof of a house.

....

    c) Door of a house.

....

Q2. Describe why it is important to reduce thermal energy losses from a home.

....

....

Q3. Double glazing is made from two panes of glass, which are separated by a gas. Describe why double installing double glazing will limit thermal energy loss from the windows.

....

....

Q4. State a way, other than double glazing, of reducing thermal energy loss through windows.

....

Q5. Takeaway containers often come in silvered aluminium containers. Describe why this limits thermal energy loss due to radiation.

....

....

Q6. Two metal bottles contain a cold liquid. One of the bottles is coloured black, the other is silver. Explain which one will keep the liquid cooler for longer.

....

....

Q7. The following statements are either true or false. State which are true and which are false.

    a) There are no particles in a vacuum.

....

    b) Plastic is a good conductor.

....

Q8. Cavity wall insulation can be made of foam, which contains trapped air bubbles. Explain why this is a good insulator.

....

....

Forces

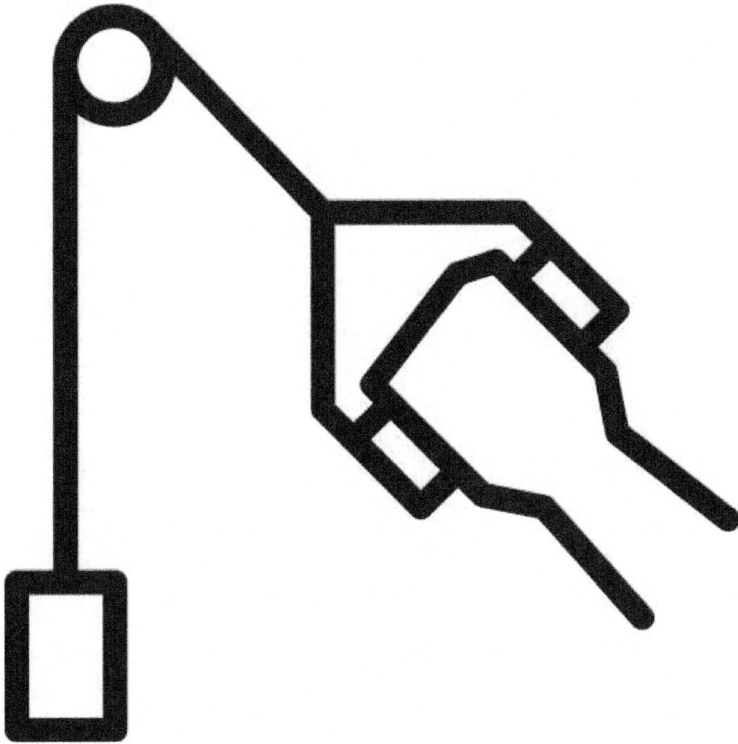

and motion

Introduction to forces

A force is a push, a pull or a twist. Forces change the **speed, direction or shape** of an object.

The unit of a force is the **Newton (N)** and forces are measured using **Newton meters**.

Forces may be represented by **arrows** in diagrams. They are drawn showing the direction the force is acting. The longer the arrow, the larger the size of the force.

The motion of an object will depend on the **resultant force**. This is calculated by combining the forces, taking their direction into account.

If two forces are in the same direction, then we calculate the resultant force by adding the forces together.

100 N ⇨ 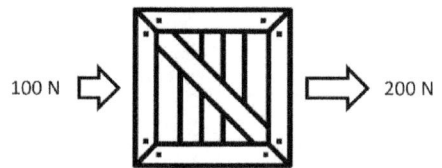 ⇨ 200 N

In the example to the right, the 100 N force and the 200 N force are both acting in the same direction (to the right). The resultant force on the crate is therefore equal to 300 N.

It is also important to write the direction the force acts. We would therefore write our final resultant force as 300 N to the right. This means that the crate will **accelerate** to the right.

If two forces are in opposite directions, then you subtract one from the other.

100 N ⇦ 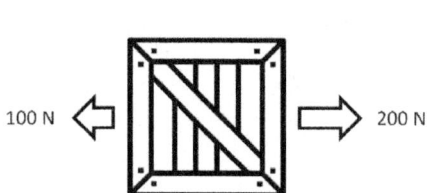 ⇨ 200 N

In the example to the left, the 100 N force and the 200 N force are acting in opposite directions. Our resultant force would be 100 N to the right.

If there's a resultant force of zero, the object will either remain stationary or remain moving at the same speed. If all individual forces make a resultant force of zero, we say the forces are **balanced**.

For example, the weight and the reaction force on the car below are **balanced**.

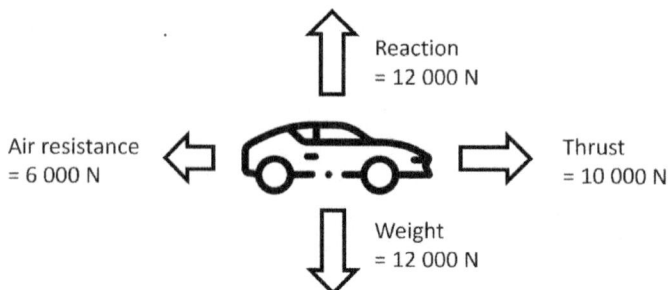

Reaction
= 12 000 N

Air resistance
= 6 000 N

Thrust
= 10 000 N

Weight
= 12 000 N

The thrust and the air resistance forces are **unbalanced** and there is a **resultant force** of 4 000 N to the right.

As there's a resultant force, the car will therefore **accelerate** to the right.

Q1. State what we use to measure the size of a force.

Newton Meter

Q2. State the unit of a force.

Newtons

Q3. Two people are competing in a tug of war. Use the force diagram to the right to answer the questions:

600 N ⟸ 👤👤 ⟹ 400 N

a) State whether the forces are balanced.

_no_

b) Calculate the resultant force.

_200 N_

Q4. A lorry is travelling on the motorway. Use the force diagram to the right to answer the questions:

Air resistance = 5 000 N ⟸ 🚚 ⟹ Thrust = 6 000 N

a) State whether the forces are balanced.

_n o_

b) Calculate the resultant force.

_1000 N_

c) State what will happen to the lorry.

It will go forward

Q5. An aeroplane is on a flight. Use the force diagram to the right to answer the questions:

Air resistance = 50 000 N ⟸ ✈ ⟹ Thrust = 50 000 N

a) State whether the forces are balanced.

b) Calculate the resultant force.

c) State what will happen to the aeroplane.

Q6. A force diagram for a boat is shown.

Resistive forces = 6 000 N ⟸ 🚤 ⟹ Thrust = 4 000 N

a) State whether the forces are balanced.

b) Calculate the resultant force.

c) State what will happen to the boat.

Types of force

There are two categories of force – those that are **contact** forces and those that are **non-contact** forces.

A **contact force** is one that acts when two objects are physically touching each other. Conversely, a **non-contact** force acts between objects that are not touching each other. Some examples are in the table below:

Name	Description	Examples
Air resistance	Contact force caused when an object travels through air. Air resistance acts against the direction of motion.	A skydiver falling through the air.
Friction	Contact force caused by two objects rubbing together. Friction also acts against the direction of motion.	Friction between somebody's shoes and the ground.
Gravitational	Attractive non-contact force. Any two objects with mass experience gravitational forces towards each other.	The Earth experiences a gravitational force as it orbits around the Sun.
Magnetic	Non-contact force caused by magnetic fields. Can be attractive or repulsive. For more on magnetic forces see page 72.	Two magnets being held near each other.
Normal reaction	This is a contact force that is in opposition to another force. It acts at 90 degrees to the surface of the object.	As we exert our weight on the ground, the ground exerts an equal and opposite reaction force.
Tension	A contact force in a rope or cable being pulled.	A rope that is being pulled.
Thrust	A contact force produced by an engine or rocket.	The forwards force of a car.
Upthrust	Upwards contact force that allows objects to float	A boat floating on water.
Weight	Non-contact force due to gravity.	All objects on Earth have a downwards weight.

Q1. The following statements are either true or false. State which are true and which are false.

a) Friction is a non-contact force.

False

b) Weight is a contact force.

True

c) Thrust is the force that allows objects to float.

False

d) Air resistance acts against the direction of motion.

True

Q2. Describe what a contact force is.

When it's a force that requires ~~to~~ physical contact. ~~to~~

Q3. State two examples of a contact force.

Friction, weight

Q4. Describe what a non-contact force is.

when ~~it~~ it's a force that doesn't require physical contact.

Q5. State two examples of a non-contact force.

Gravitational, electric

Q6. The diagram to the left shows a skydiver falling through the air. Label the downwards force and the upwards force.

Q7. The downwards and the upwards force on the skydiver are balanced.

a) Describe what it means to say that two forces are balanced.

b) State what will happen to the speed of the skydiver.

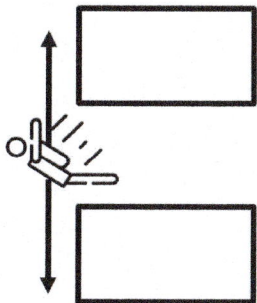

Q8. The diagram to the right shows a car driving along a road. Label the forces.

Q9. The forwards force is greater than the backwards force. State what will happen to the speed of the car.

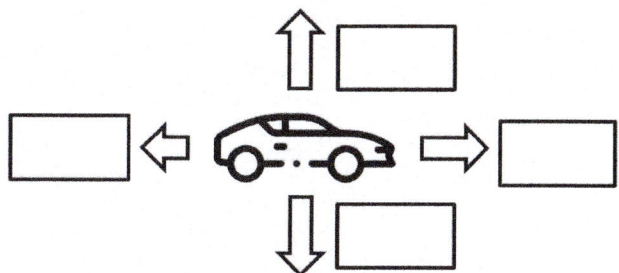

Hooke's law

When a force is applied to a spring, the spring **extends** (increases in length) or **compresses** (decreases in length). The extension or compression depends on the size of the force applied.

The diagram to the right shows a spring with different extensions. In the first diagram there is no mass hung from the spring and so there is no extension.

The second diagram shows a mass hung from the spring, and this gives an extension of x.

This extension is doubled to 2x when two of the same masses are hung from the spring. This is shown in the third diagram.

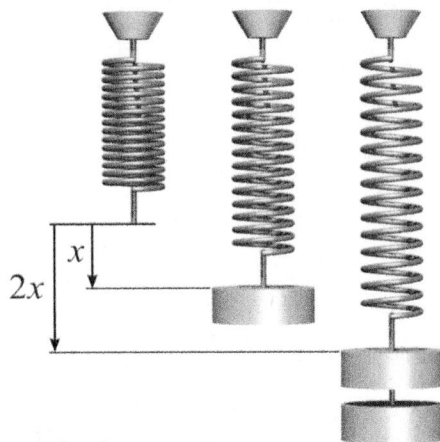

By Svjo - Own work, CC BY-SA 3.0, https://commons.wikimedia.org/w/index.php?curid=253 98333

This is summarised in Hooke's law:

The extension of a spring is directly proportional to the force applied to it.

This also leads to the following equation

Force = Spring constant × Extension   which in symbols is   **F = k × e**

where F is the **force** with units of **Newtons** (N)

k is the **spring constant** with units of **Newtons per metre** (N/m)

e is the **extension** with units of **metres** (m).

The spring constant is a measure of how much force is needed to extend the spring by one metre.

The higher the spring constant, the more force is needed to stretch the spring by the same amount.

This is shown in the diagram to the right. Note how the force is directly proportional to the extension.

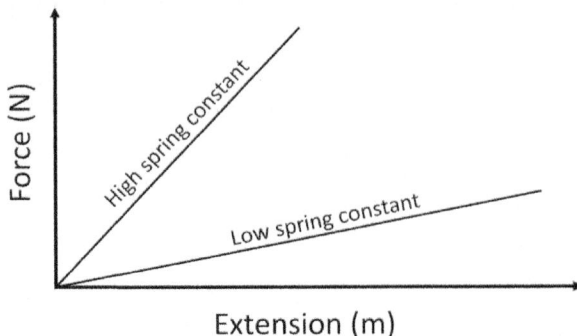

Q1. State the unit of a force. ....

Q2. State the unit of the spring constant. ....

Q3. State the unit of extension. ....

Q4. Describe how the extension of a spring is related to the force applied to it.

....

....

Q5. A spring with a spring constant of 4 N/m is extended by 0.1 m when a force is applied to it. Calculate the force applied to the spring.

Force = Spring constant × Extension
= 4 N/m × 0.1 m
= _____ **N**

Q6. A rubber band with a spring constant of 10 N/m is extended by 0.2 m when a force is applied to it. Calculate the force applied to the spring.

Force = Spring constant × Extension
= _____ _____ × _____ __
= _____ __

Q7. A spring with a spring constant of 20 N/m is compressed by 0.05 m when a force is applied to it. Calculate the force applied to the spring.

Force = _____ × _____
= _____ _____ × _____ __
= _____ __

Q8. The same force is applied to two different springs. Spring X has a high spring constant and Spring Y has a low spring constant. State which spring will have the larger extension.

....

Q9. A rubber band has a spring constant of 60 N/m and is pulled with a force of 15 N. Calculate the extension of the rubber band.

Extension = Force ÷ Spring constant
= _____ __ ÷ _____ _____
= _____ __

Q10. A spring has a spring constant of 200 N/m and is compressed by 0.04 m when a force is applied to it. Calculate the force applied to the spring.

....

....

Q11. A rubber band has a spring constant of 15 N/m and is pulled with a force of 0.3 N. Calculate the extension of the rubber band.

....

....

Moments

A **moment** is a turning force. The equation to calculate a moment is

Moment = Force × Distance

In this equation, the distance (measured in metres) is the **perpendicular distance to the pivot**.

Force applied

Forces are measured in **Newtons** (N) and moments are therefore measured in **Newton metres** (Nm).

The diagram to the right shows one example use of a turning force. A spanner is used as a **force-multiplier**. This means that by applying a force at a greater distance, we only need to apply a smaller force to turn the bolt.

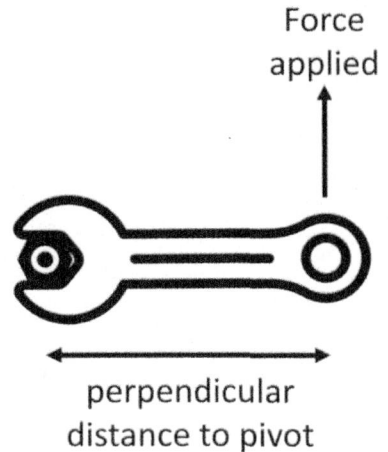

perpendicular distance to pivot

The principle of moments tells us that:

An object is balanced when the sum of the clockwise moments about a point are equal to the sum of the anticlockwise moments about the point.

We can use this when talking about objects being balanced or unbalanced on a seesaw.

Example question:

Using the diagram to the right, state whether the seesaw is balanced or not.

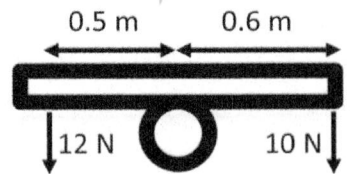

0.5 m   0.6 m

12 N   10 N

Step 1. Calculate clockwise moments.

Moment = 10 × 0.6 = 6 Nm

Step 2. Calculate anticlockwise moments.

Moment = 12 × 0.5 = 6 Nm

Step 3. Conclusion. If the size of the moments is equal; then the seesaw is balanced.

Yes, the seesaw is balanced.

Q1. State the equation that links a moment, force and perpendicular distance to pivot.

force = time x distance from pivot

Q2. State the units of a moment, force and distance.

N/m

Q3. Describe the principle of moments.

Clockwise / Anticlockwise

Q4. Using the diagrams below, calculate the moment applied to each of the bolts:

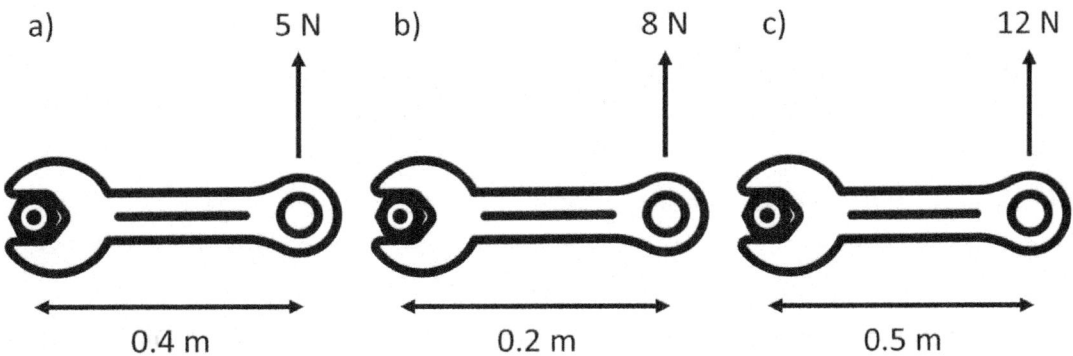

a)   5 N   b)   8 N   c)   12 N

0.4 m   0.2 m   0.5 m

a) 2Nm

b) 1.6Nm

c) 6Nm

Q5. Using the diagram to the right, state whether the seesaw is balanced or not.

no it's not because on the left it's 4N/m and on the right it's 7.2N/m

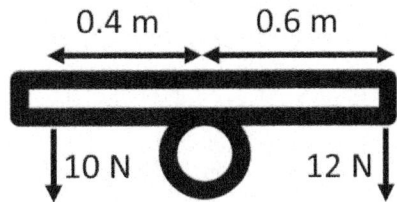

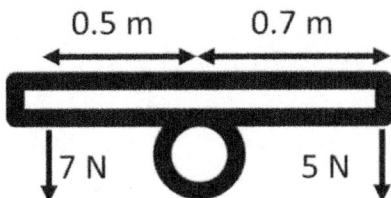

0.4 m   0.6 m

10 N   12 N

0.5 m   0.7 m

7 N   5 N

Q6. Using the diagram to the left, state whether the seesaw is balanced or not.

yes, they are equal equalibrium

Pressure

Pressure is a measure of how much **force** is applied over a given **area**.

The diagram to the right shows three holes in a bottle full of water.

The hole at the top of the bottle only has a small weight of water above it and so the pressure of the water is comparatively small at this point. Therefore water is only pushed out of the bottle at a relatively low speed.

The hole in the middle of the bottle has more weight of water above it, and therefore experiences a larger pressure. This, in turn, pushes water out of the bottle at a higher speed.

The hole at the bottom of the bottle has the most weight of water above it, and experiences the largest pressure. This explains why water is pushed out of the bottle at the highest speed.

This doesn't only apply to water and liquids, but also to atmospheric pressure. Atmospheric pressure decreases as we increase in height above Earth's surface. This is because as we go further from the Earth's surface there's less weight of air above us.

Pressure can be calculated using the equation:

$$\text{Pressure} = \text{Force} \div \text{Area}$$

Force is measured in **Newtons**, while **area** is measured in **metres squared** (m^2). The unit of pressure is a **Pascal** (Pa), which is the same as one Newton per metre squared (N/m^2).

Example question:

A force of 500 N is applied over an area of 0.25 m^2. Calculate the pressure.

Step 1. Write down equation: Pressure = Force ÷ Area

Step 2. Insert variables into equation: = 500 N ÷ 0.25 m^2

Step 3. Calculate answer. Remember units: = 2000 Pa

Q1. State the equation that links pressure, force and area.

....

Q2. State the units of pressure, force and area.

....

Q3. Describe what happens to atmospheric pressure as we go higher above the Earth's surface.

....

....

Q4. A full bottle has two holes in it, one higher than the other. State which of the two holes water will come out faster. Explain why.

....

....

Q5. A crate has a weight of 2600 N and the area of the crate's base is 2 m^2. Calculate the pressure the crate exerts on the ground.

Pressure = Force ÷ Area
= 2600 N ÷ 2 m^2
= _____ **Pa**

Q6. A book has a weight of 20 N and the area of the book is 0.02 m^2. The book is lying on a table. Calculate the pressure the book exerts on the table.

Pressure = _____ ÷ _____
= _____ **N ÷** _____ **m^2**
= _____ **Pa**

Q7. A skip has a weight of 5000 N and the area of the crate's base is 4 m^2. Calculate the pressure the skip exerts on the ground.

Pressure = _____ ÷ _____
= _____ __ ÷ _____ __
= _____ __

Q8. A person has a weight of 700 N and their shoes have a combined area of 0.04 m^2. Calculate the pressure the person exerts on the ground.

....

....

Q9. Somebody is walking in a wet field. Describe which of a high heel shoe or a trainer will sink into the ground more. Explain why.

....

....

Speed

Speed is a measure of the **distance** an object has moved in a certain **time**. When travelling in a car or an aeroplane, you might have heard of speed being measured in miles per hour (mph) or kilometres per hour (km/h).

In physics, speed is usually measured in **metres per second** (m/s).

If an object is travelling at a constant speed of 30 m/s, that means it travels a distance 30 metres every second. If an object travels at 12 m/s, it travels a distance of 12 metres every second.

The equation to calculate speed is:

Speed = Distance ÷ Time

Example question 1:

A car travels a distance of 400 m in a time of 20 seconds. Calculate the **speed** of the car.

Step 1. Write down equation:	**Speed = Distance ÷ Time**
Step 2. Insert variables into equation:	**= 400 m ÷ 20 s**
Step 3. Calculate answer. Remember units:	**= 20 m/s**

We can also be asked questions to calculate distance or time. We know that if an object travels at 30 m/s, it travels a distance of 30 m/s every second. Therefore in 2 seconds, it would travel 30 × 2 = 60 m. To calculate the distance, we multiply the speed by the time:

Distance = Speed × Time.

Example question 2:

An athlete runs a race at an average speed of 8 m/s. The athlete takes a time of 50 seconds to complete the race. Calculate the **distance** of the race.

Step 1. Write down equation:	**Speed = Distance ÷ Time**
Step 2. Insert variables into equation:	**8 = Distance ÷ 50**
Step 3. Rearrange equation:	**Distance = 8 × 50**
Step 3. Calculate answer. Remember units:	**= 400 m**

We can also look at the speed of one object relative to another. For example, take a car that is travelling at 30 m/s and a train is travelling 20 m/s faster than the car.

The train is therefore moving at a speed of 50 m/s, you just add the speeds together to get the speed of the train.

Q1. Describe what speed is.

....

Q2. An object is travelling at a constant speed of 20 m/s. Calculate how far the object travels every second.

....

Q3. An object is travelling at a constant speed of 8 m/s. Calculate how far the objects travel every second.

....

Q4. A car is travelling at a speed of 20 m/s, and a train is travelling 10 m/s faster than the car. State the speed of the train.

....

Q5. State the equation to calculate speed.

....

Q6. A cyclist travels a distance of 120 m in a time of 20 seconds. Calculate the speed of the cyclist.

Speed = Distance ÷ Time
        = 120 m ÷ 20 s
        = _____ m/s

Q7. A runner travels a distance of 1500 m in a time of 500 s. Calculate the speed of the runner.

Speed = Distance ÷ Time
        = _____ __ ÷ ___ __
        = _____ m/s

Q8. Someone walking their dog travels a distance of 1200 m in a time of 1000 seconds. Calculate the speed of the dog walker.

Speed = _____ ÷ _____
        = _____ __ ÷ ___ __
        = _____ ___

Q9. A sound wave travels a distance of 686 m in a time of 2 seconds. Calculate the speed of sound.

....

Q10. Light travels a distance of 4 500 000 000 m in a time of 15 seconds. Calculate the speed of light.

....

Q11. A car travels at a speed of 25 m/s for a time of 400 s. Calculate the distance travelled by the car.

Speed = Distance ÷ Time
        25 = Distance ÷ 400
    Distance = ___ × ____
        = _____ m

Q12. A motorbike travels at a constant speed of 40 m/s for a time of 20 s. Calculate the distance travelled by the motorbike.

....

Distance-time graphs

Distance-time graphs are used to represent the journey of an object that is travelling.

The **gradient** (or steepness) of a distance-time graph gives the speed of the object.

An example distance-time graph is shown to the right, where two joggers are shown.

The steeper the gradient of a distance-time graph the greater the speed of the object.

Because of this, we can tell which jogger is travelling at a higher speed.

Mathematically, the gradient is calculated by using the equation:

$$\text{gradient} = \frac{\text{change on y axis}}{\text{change on x axis}} = \frac{\Delta y}{\Delta x}$$

For distance-time graphs, Δy is the distance travelled and Δx is the time taken to travel that distance. This makes sense, because we already know the equation to calculate speed is:

Speed = Distance ÷ Time

The faster jogger in the diagram above travels a distance of 25 m in a time of 5 s. We can therefore calculate their speed to be 5 m/s.

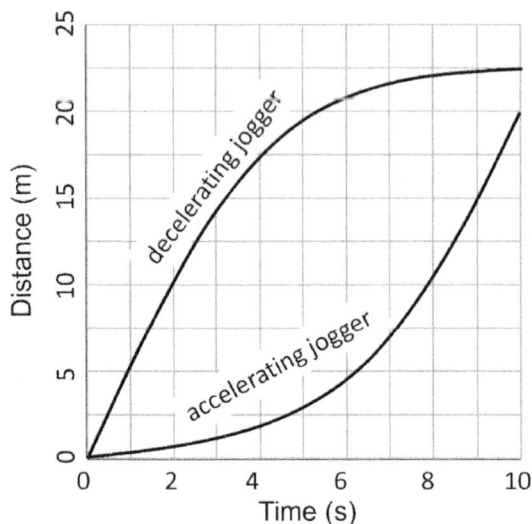

The slower jogger travels a distance of 25 m in a time of 10 s. We can therefore calculate their speed to be 2.5 m/s.

The diagram to the left shows two more distance time graphs.

The higher graph shows a jogger that is decelerating. We know the jogger is decelerating because the gradient of the graph is reducing over time.

The lower graph shows a jogger that is accelerating. We know this because the gradient of the graph is increasing over time.

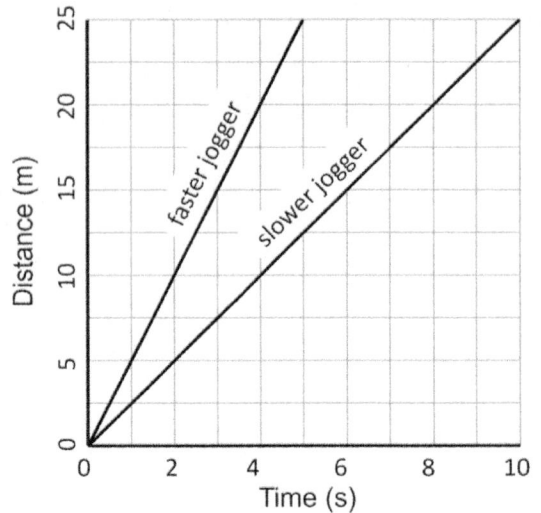

Q1. State what the gradient of a distance-time graph represents.

How fast an object is going.

Q2. State the equation for speed.

$S = \frac{d}{t}$

Q3. Using the distance-time graphs below, calculate the speed of each of the objects:

5m/s
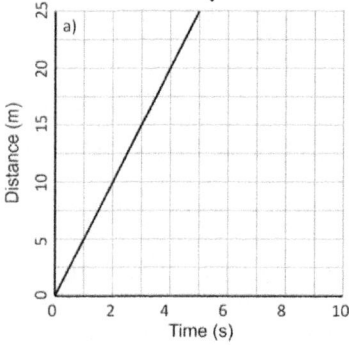

1.5/
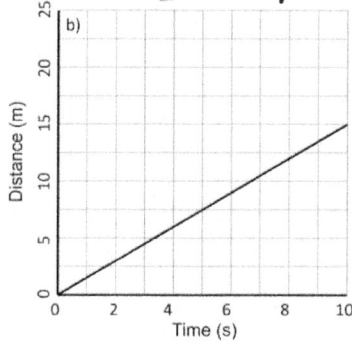

2m/s
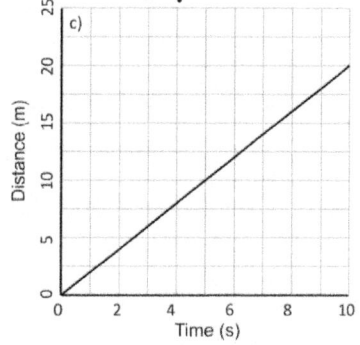

4m/s
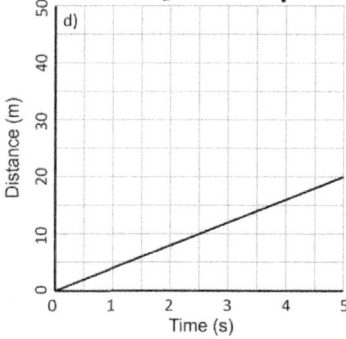

12.5mk
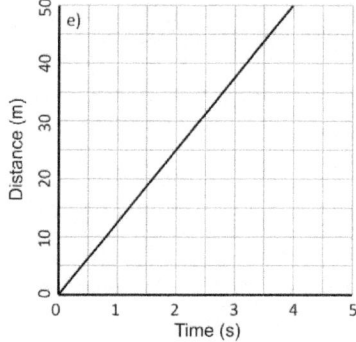

9m/s
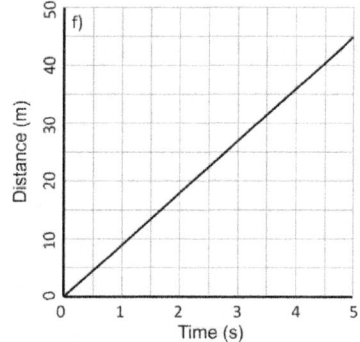

a) ....

b) ....

c) ....

d) ....

e) ....

f) ....

Terminal velocity

When a skydiver jumps out of an aeroplane they **accelerate**. Their acceleration (the rate at which they speed up) is not constant throughout the skydive. We use **Newton's laws** to describe the motion of objects:

Newton's first law: The speed of an object will remain the same unless a resultant force acts on the object. This includes if an object is initially stationary. If there is no resultant force acting on a stationary object, it will remain stationary.

Newton's second law: The acceleration of an object is proportional to the resultant force on the object. The larger the resultant force, the larger the acceleration of the object.

Newton's third law: If object A exerts a force on object B, then object B exerts a force of equal size and opposite direction on object A.

The diagram to the right shows the force diagrams of a skydiver at different stages in their skydive:

1. The skydiver has just jumped out of the aeroplane and hasn't quite started falling yet. The only force acting on the skydiver is their weight. As this is the only force, the skydiver accelerates.
2. As the skydiver increases in speed, the air resistance increases. The **resultant force** downwards decreases, **and according to Newton's second** law the acceleration downwards must also decrease.
3. Eventually, when the skydiver reaches a certain speed, the air resistance is equal to the weight. As the forces are balanced, there is no **resultant force**. Due to Newton's first law, the speed of the skydiver remains the same. The acceleration is zero. The speed is called the **terminal** (maximum) **velocity**.
4. When the skydiver opens their parachute, they have a much larger **surface area.** This dramatically increases the air resistance and there is a **resultant force** upwards. This means the skydiver decelerates.
5. As the skydiver slows down, the air resistance decreases until it is equal to the weight again. The forces are **balanced** and the skydiver reaches a second (slower) terminal velocity.

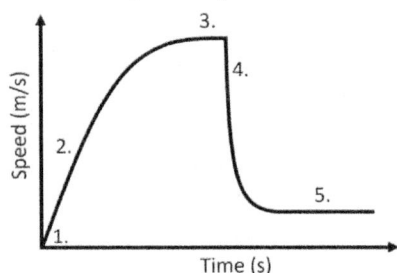

These stages are also shown in the graph to the left. Here, the speeds of the skydiver at shown at each stage. Note the terminal velocities at stages 3 and 5.

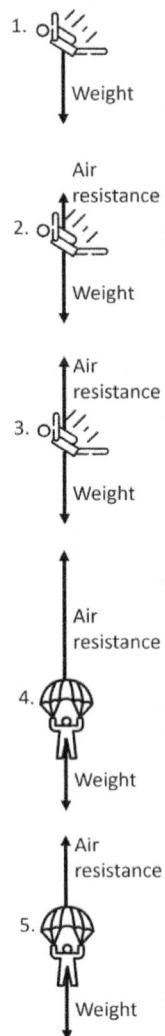

Q1. State what happens to air resistance as the speed of an object increases.

....

Q2. A car is travelling at a speed of 70 mph on the motorway. All the forces on the car are balanced. State what happens to the speed of the car.

....

Q3. The car now has a resultant force forwards. State what happens to the speed of the car.

....

Q4. Using the diagram to the right, state and explain whether the skydiver will be accelerating, decelerating, or falling at a constant speed.

....

....

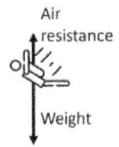

Q5. Using the diagram to the right, state and explain whether the skydiver will be accelerating, decelerating, or falling at a constant speed.

....

....

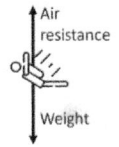

Q6. Using the diagram to the right, state and explain whether the skydiver will be accelerating, decelerating, or falling at a constant speed.

....

....

Q7. Explain how a skydiver reaches a terminal velocity.

....

....

....

Q8. State and explain what happens to the air resistance on a skydiver straight after they open their parachute.

....

....

Q9. For the questions below, use the speed-time graph of a skydiver to the right.

a) Annotate with an "A" where the skydiver is accelerating.
b) Annotate with a "T" two regions of terminal velocity.
c) Annotate with a "P" the time when the parachute is opened.

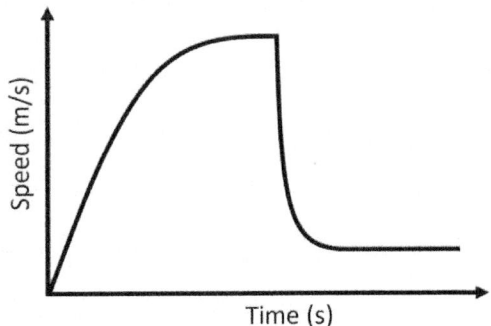

Waves

Introduction to waves

Waves transfer energy from one place to another, without transferring any matter.

There are two types of wave; **longitudinal** and **transverse**.

Both longitudinal and transverse waves are caused by **vibrations**. However, transverse waves are caused by a vibration that is **perpendicular** to the direction of wave travel. Longitudinal waves are caused by a vibration that is **parallel** to the direction of wave travel.

These waves are shown below, where a slinky is being used to demonstrate transverse and longitudinal waves in images a) and b) respectively.

Note two areas are labelled on the longitudinal wave. A **compression** is where particles in the wave are closest together, and a **rarefaction** is where they are furthest apart.

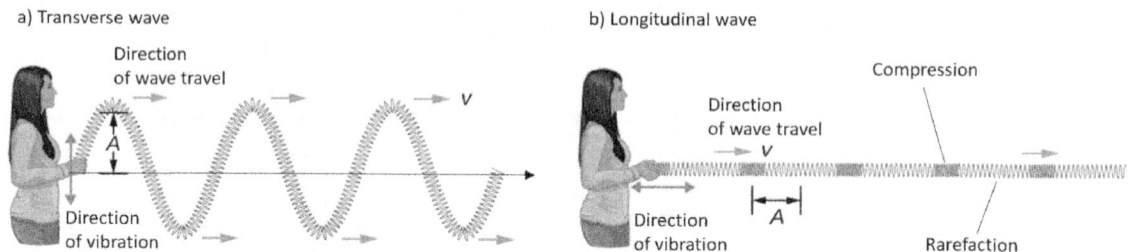

a) Transverse wave

b) Longitudinal wave

Adapted from original image at https://openstax.org/books/university-physics-volume-1/pages/1-introduction. Licensed under CC BY.

A diagram of a transverse wave is also shown below, including some key terminology:

Displacement	How far a point on the wave is from the rest position.
Wavelength	Distance from peak to peak (or any complete wave cycle).
Amplitude	Maximum displacement of wave.

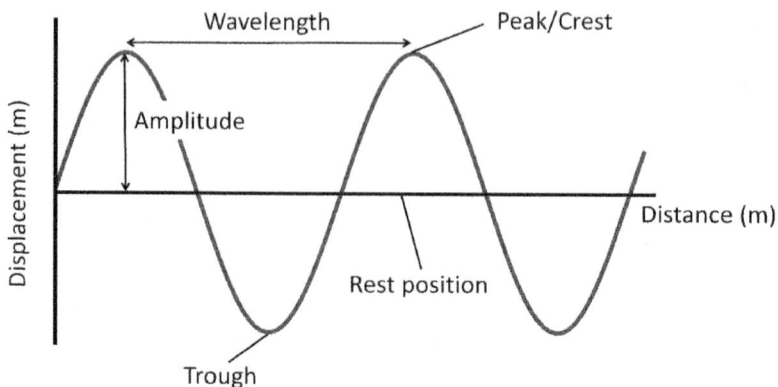

Q1. The following statements are either true or false. State which are true and which are false.

a) A wave transfers energy from one place to another.

....

b) A wave transfers matter from one place to another.

....

c) Vibrations are the cause of both longitudinal and transverse waves.

....

d) In a longitudinal wave, a compression is where particles in the wave are closest together.

....

e) In a transverse wave, the vibration that causes the wave is parallel to the direction of wave travel.

....

Q2. Label the diagram of the transverse wave below.

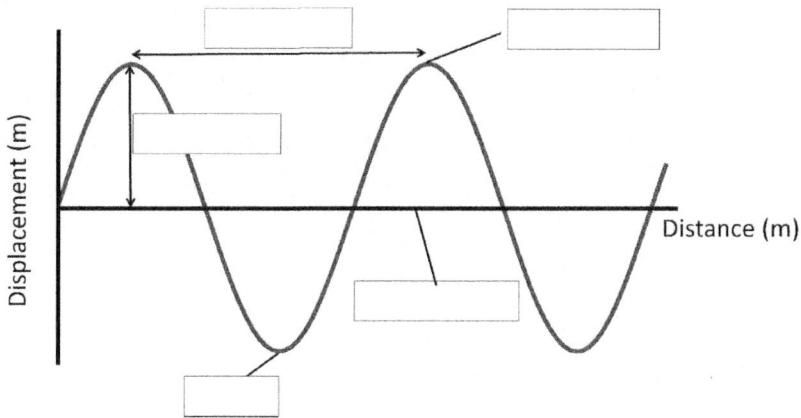

Q3. Describe what a rarefaction is in a longitudinal wave.

....

....

Q4. Describe a similarity between a longitudinal wave and a transverse wave.

....

....

Q5. Describe the difference between a longitudinal wave and a transverse wave.

....

....

....

....

Sound

An object that is **vibrating** makes a sound wave. The object vibrates air particles and these particles collide with other air particles and **transfer energy**. Sound is a **longitudinal** wave. This means the vibrations that cause the sound wave are **parallel** to the direction of wave travel.

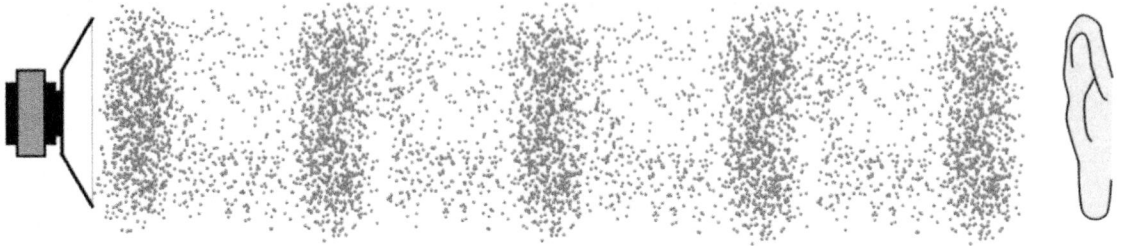

By Pluke - Own work, CC0, https://commons.wikimedia.org/w/index.php?curid=18413169

The diagram above shows the cone of a speaker vibrating and forming a sound wave in air. **Compressions** are formed when the air particles are close together. **Rarefactions** are formed where air particles are further apart. The **wavelength** is the distance between one compression and the next (or one rarefaction and the next).

The **frequency** of a sound wave (measured in units of **Hertz**) is related to the **pitch** of a sound wave. The higher the frequency, the higher the pitch. The frequency is a measure of how many sound waves pass a point every second. If 200 sound waves pass a point every second, then the frequency is 200 Hz.

The **amplitude** of a sound wave is related to the **volume**. The larger the amplitude, the louder the sound wave will be.

We can turn a sound wave into an electrical signal by using a **microphone**. The sound wave vibrates a **diaphragm** in the microphone and produces an electrical signal. This electrical signal can be viewed on an **oscilloscope**.

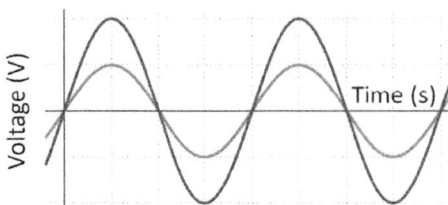

Adapted from crh23, CC BY-SA 4.0
<https://creativecommons.org/licenses/by-sa/4.0>, via
Wikimedia Commons

The diagram to the left shows two example traces from a microphone that would be viewed on an oscilloscope screen. They both have the same frequency, but one has a larger amplitude than the other. The amplitude is related to the volume of the sound wave.

Our ears detect sound waves in a similar way, the sound waves vibrate our **ear drum**. These vibrations are turned into electrical signals which are sent to the brain and interpreted as a sound.

Q1. State what causes a sound wave.

....

Q2. State the definition of a longitudinal wave.

....

Q3. The auditory range for humans is any frequency between 20 and 20 000 Hz. State the definition of frequency.

....

Q4. A sound wave with a frequency above 20 000 Hz is called ultrasound. How many waves pass a point every second for an ultrasound wave with frequency 20 000 Hz?

....

Q5. Sound waves consist of compressions and rarefactions. Describe the difference between a compression and a rarefaction.

....

....

....

Q6. The following statements are either true or false. State which are true and which are false.

    a) The wavelength is the distance between a compression and a rarefaction.

....

    b) The higher the frequency of a sound wave, the louder it is.

....

    c) The lower the amplitude of a sound wave, the quieter it is.

....

    d) A microphone is used to turn a sound wave into an electrical signal.

....

Q7. A microphone and an oscilloscope is used to produce a trace of a sound wave. On the axes below, draw two traces of sound waves. They should both have the same amplitude, but one should have a higher frequency than the other.

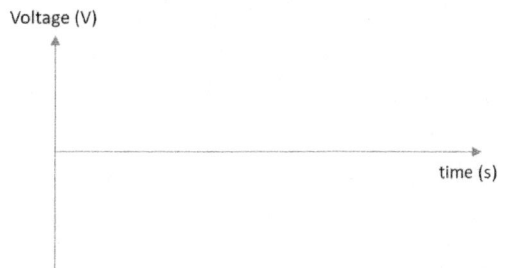

Voltage (V)

time (s)

Voltage (V)

time (s)

Speed of sound

Sound waves need particles (a **medium**) to travel. Sound cannot travel in a **vacuum** as there are no particles in a vacuum.

The speed of sound in air is approximately 340 m/s (although this depends on the pressure and temperature of the air).

Sound travels faster in liquids and solids than in air. For example, the speed of sound in water is approximately 1500 m/s and the speed of sound in steel is over 3000 m/s.

This is because the particles in a gas are far apart, while the particles in a liquid or solid are closer together. The vibrations are therefore transferred more quickly.

Usually, sound travels slowest in gases and fastest in solids.

If we wanted to measure the speed of sound in air, we can use an **echo**. An echo is a **reflection** of a sound wave from a surface.

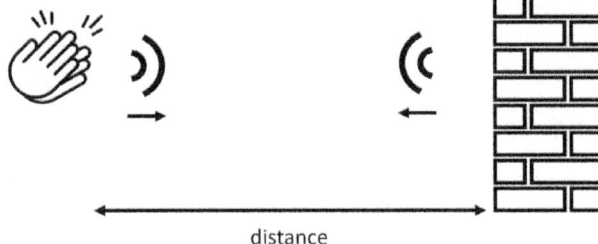

The following method could be used to measure the speed of sound:

distance

1. Stand at least 50 metres from a wall/cliff. To measure this distance use either a measuring tape, or a trundle wheel.

2. Make a loud sound (for example using a clap).

3. Using a **stopwatch**, measure the time for sound to return.

4. Calculate speed by using **Speed = Total distance ÷ Time**.

5. Repeat three times and take average.

Remember the sound wave travels to the wall and back, so the total distance is the distance to the wall multiplied by two.

We could get a more accurate reading for the speed of sound by using a microphone attached to an oscilloscope. The oscilloscope would show a pulse for when the initial sound is made and when the reflected sound returns. This would remove error due to **human reaction time**.

When sound is reflected from a **medium** some sound is **absorbed**. This means that not all of the sound will be **reflected** back.

Q1. The following statements are either true or false. State which are true and which are false.

a) Sound waves can travel through a vacuum.

False ✓

b) Sound usually travels faster through a solid than through air.

True ✓

c) The equation to calculate speed of sound is speed = total distance × time.

False ✓

Q2. Somebody is trying to measure the speed of sound. They stand a distance of 50 metres from a wall and clap. They hear an echo a time of 0.40 seconds later. Calculate the speed of sound.

50 ÷ 0.4

Q3. The answer to question 2 is less than the actual speed of sound. This is because of human reaction time. Explain why human reaction time has led to a speed of sound that is lower than expected.

The time should be shorter

Q4. Rearrange the equation for speed to give an equation for distance.

Q5. Human reaction time is usually around 250 ms (0.25 seconds). Calculate how far a sound wave travels in that time. Take the speed of sound to be 340 m/s.

Q6. Bats use something called echolocation to locate objects around them. Echolocation works by the bat sending a sound wave outwards and using the echo to estimate how far an object is away from them. One bat detects an echo a time of 0.80 seconds after the sound wave was sent. Calculate how far away the object is from the bat. Take the speed of sound to be 340 m/s.

136

Water waves and superposition

The diagram to the right shows **water waves** being formed in a **ripple tank**. A motor is connected to a **dipper** and makes the dipper vibrate up and down in the water. Each time the dipper does this a water wave is formed.

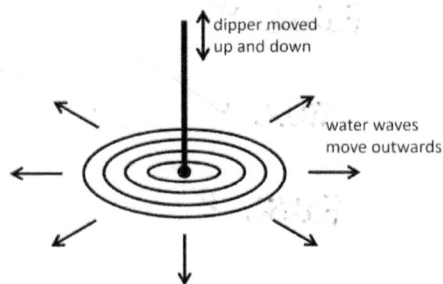

dipper moved up and down

water waves move outwards

Like all waves, water waves transfer energy without transferring matter.

Water waves are one example of a **transverse** wave. Transverse waves are caused by a vibration that is **perpendicular** to the direction of wave travel. Note how the dipper moves up and down, but the water waves move **perpendicularly** in every direction outwards.

Waves also interact with each other if one wave passes through another. This is called **superposition**. This occurs for both water waves and other types of wave.

We've previously learnt that the displacement of a wave is the distance a particle in the wave has moved from its rest position. When superposition occurs, the displacements of the waves add together.

Two examples of superposition are shown in the diagram below.

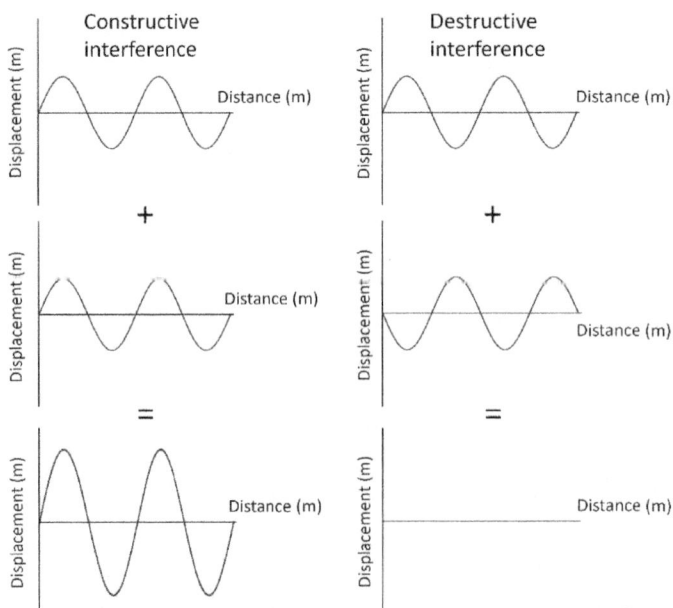

Constructive interference

Destructive interference

+

+

=

=

When two peaks of a wave arrive at one place at the same time, they add. The amplitude of the combined wave is more than each individual wave. This is shown on the left hand side of the diagram.

When a peak of a wave arrives at one place at the same time as the trough of another wave, they cancel. The amplitude of the combined wave is less than each individual wave. This is shown on the right hand part of the diagram.

More generally, if the displacements of the two waves are the same sign (i.e. both positive) then they add together. If they are opposite signs, they subtract.

Q1. The following statements are either true or false. State which are true and which are false.

a) Water waves are longitudinal.

b) Longitudinal waves are caused by a vibration that is perpendicular to the direction of wave travel.

c) Water waves transfer energy without transferring matter.

d) When two waves overlap, superposition occurs.

Q2. State one example of a transverse wave.

Q3. Describe how transverse waves are formed.

Q4. The two waves below undergo superposition. On the blank axes to the right, draw the combined wave.

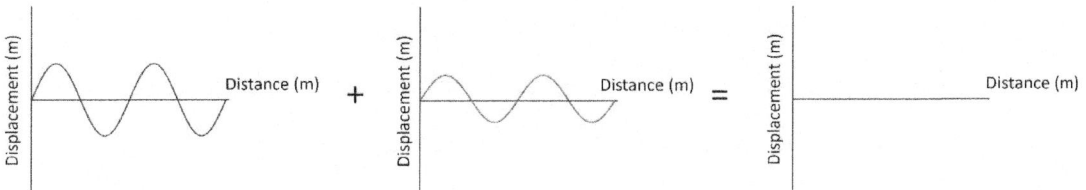

Q5. The two waves below undergo superposition. On the blank axes to the right, draw the combined wave.

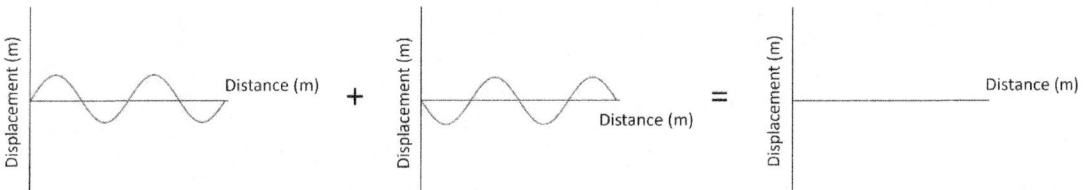

Q6. The two waves below undergo superposition. On the blank axes to the right, draw the combined wave.

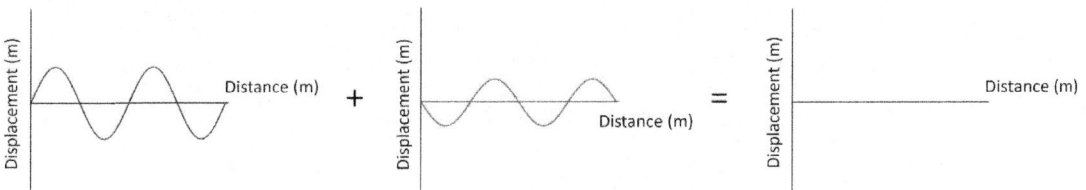

Reflection

We can see ourselves in a mirror because mirrors **reflect** light.

Light is another example of a **transverse** wave and travels at 300 000 000 m/s (the speed of light). Transverse waves are caused by a vibration that is **perpendicular** to the direction of wave travel.

Specular reflections happen when rays of light are reflected from a very smooth surface like a mirror. The diagram below shows **specular** reflection of light from a mirror.

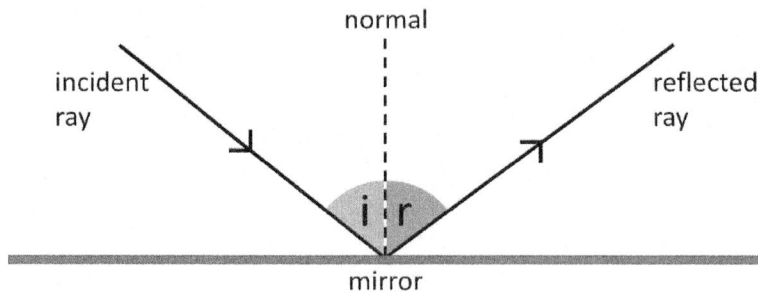

The ray going into the mirror is called the **incident ray**. The **angle of incidence** is the angle that this ray makes to the **normal**. The normal is an imaginary line that we draw at an angle of 90° to the mirror. An arrow shows the direction of the ray.

The **angle of refraction** is also measured between the **reflected ray** and the normal.

This diagram also shows the **law of reflection**. The law of reflection says that:

The angle of incidence is equal to the angle of reflection.

This law doesn't only apply to light, but also to other waves. For example, light is part of a family of seven transverse waves in the **electromagnetic spectrum.**

If rays of light are shone onto a surface that isn't smooth, then a **diffuse reflection** happens.

In a diffuse reflection, rays are reflected at many angles. The angle of incidence is still equal to the angle of reflection; it's just the surface isn't smooth and points in different directions.

This is shown in the diagram to the right.

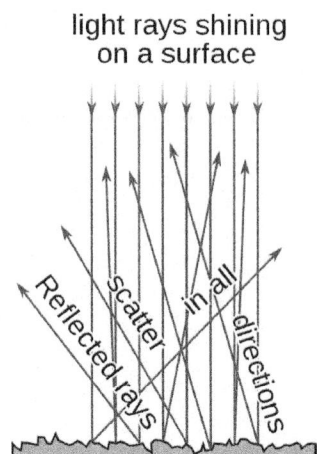

Jeff Dahl, CC BY-SA 3.0 <https://creativecommons.org/licenses /by-sa/3.0>, via Wikimedia Commons

Q1. The following statements are either true or false. State which are true and which are false.

a) Light is a transverse wave.

....

b) Transverse waves are caused by a vibration that is perpendicular to the direction of wave travel.

....

c) Diffuse reflections happen when rays of light are reflected from a very smooth surface.

....

d) In a diffuse reflection, the angle of incidence is not always equal to the angle of reflection.

....

e) Light is shone onto a mirror. The angle of incidence is measured from the incident ray to the mirror.

....

f) Only light obeys the law of reflection.

....

Q2. State the speed of light.

....

Q3. State the law of reflection.

....

....

Q4. Describe the difference between a specular and a diffuse reflection.

....

....

Q5. The diagram of reflection below is incomplete. Draw the reflected ray and label the diagram completely.

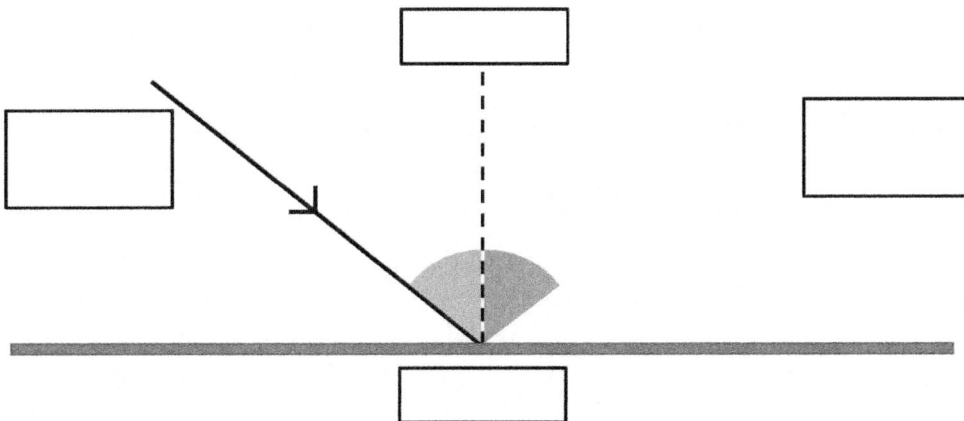

Refraction

The speed of light in a vacuum is 300 000 000 m/s. Nothing can travel faster than this. However, this speed is decreased if the light travels through a different **medium** (material). For example, the speed of light in glass is approximately 200 000 000 m/s. This is because glass has a higher **refractive index** than a vacuum. The higher the refractive index, the slower light travels through the material.

This decrease in velocity also causes two other things:

1. A decrease in wavelength of the light.
2. Unless the angle of incidence is 0°, there will be a change in direction of the light.

The frequency of light is unchanged. The diagram below shows refraction of light from air into a glass block.

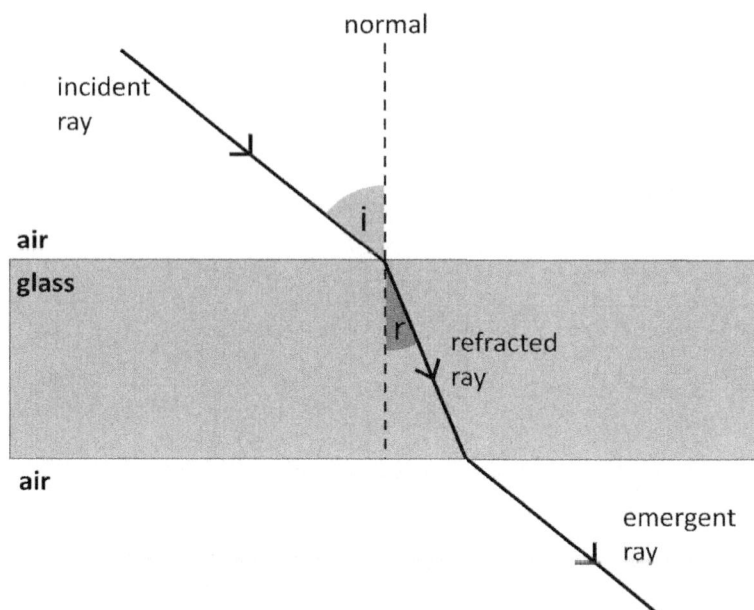

As the light passes from air into glass, it slows down as the refractive index of glass is more than the refractive index of air. The light refracts and changes direction, bending towards the normal (an imaginary line at 90° to the glass block). The angle of refraction (labelled r) is less than the angle of incidence (labelled i).

As the light exits the glass block, the opposite happens. Air has a lower refractive index than glass and so speeds up and refracts away from the normal. The ray that exits the block is called the emergent ray. The emergent ray travels in the same direction as the initial incident ray.

If the angle of incidence is 0°, then light continues in the same direction (but more slowly).

Q1. The following statements are either true or false. State which are true and which are false.

a) Light travels at the same speed in a vacuum as it does in glass.

....

b) When light goes from air into a glass block, its wavelength decreases.

....

c) When light goes from air into a glass block, the angle of refraction is less than the angle of incidence.

....

d) When light goes from air into a glass block, the frequency of the light of the light remains unchanged.

....

Q2. Complete the diagrams below by drawing the refracted ray. In part c), the incident ray is going in the same direction as the normal.

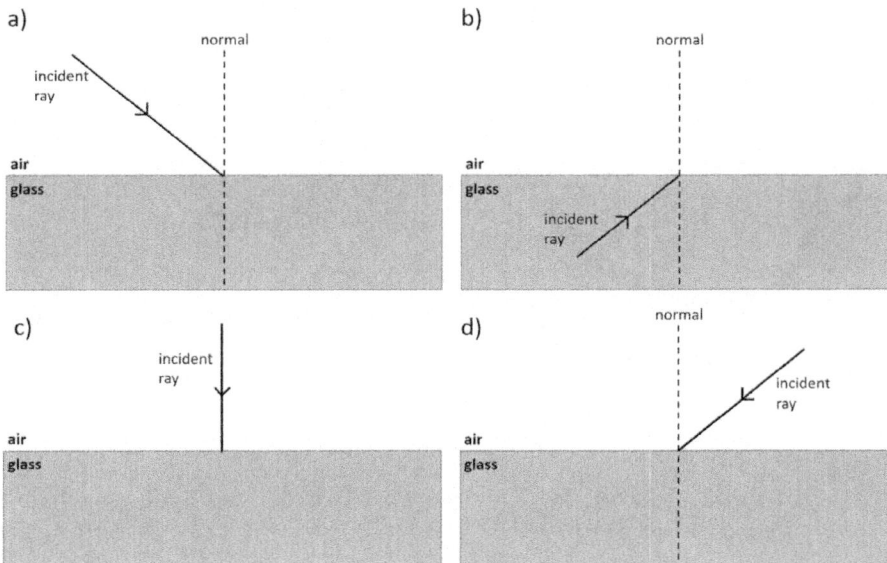

Q3. The diagram to the right shows the "bent pencil" illusion when a pencil appears to be bent when partially submerged in water. Describe why this illusion happens.

....

....

....

....

....

....

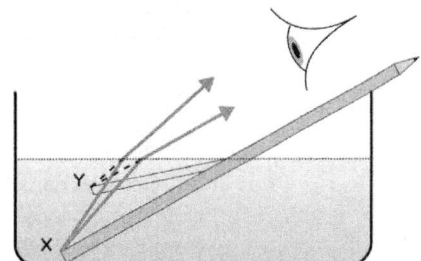

Pencil_in_a_bowl_of_water.png: Theresa Knott derivative work: Gregors (talk) ,CC BY-SA 3.0, via Wikimedia Commons

51

The human eye

The human eye contains a **convex lens**. A convex lens is wider in the middle than it is at the edges. Because of this, rays of light refract by different amounts depending on where they hit the lens. This causes the light to **converge** (come together) at a **focal point**. This is shown in the diagram to the right.

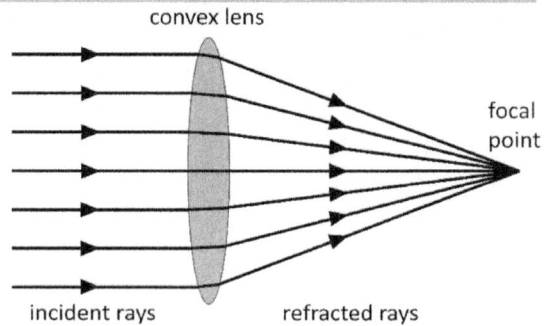

convex lens

focal point

incident rays   refracted rays

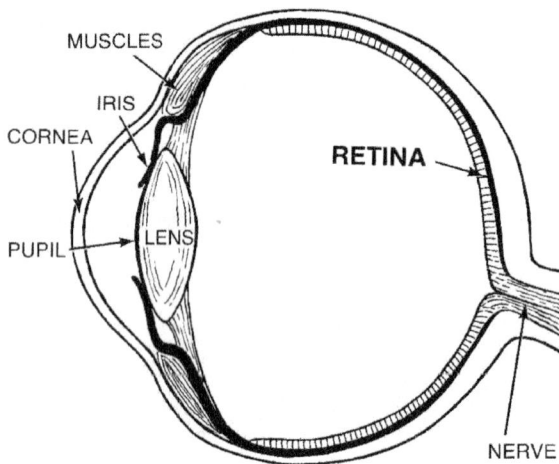

MUSCLES

IRIS

CORNEA

RETINA

PUPIL

LENS

NERVE

Pearson Scott Foresman, Public domain, via Wikimedia Commons

Convex lenses are used in objects like:

- Glasses to help people with farsightedness.
- Magnifying glasses.
- Telescopes.

The convex lens inside the eye allows for light to be focused on the back of the eye (called the retina).

A diagram of the human eye is to the left, and descriptions of each of the parts are below.

Cornea	Transparent layer at the front of the eye. Some refraction of light occurs here.
Retina	Contains cells that can detect light and colour. It is sensitive to light that is too bright and can be damaged.
Lens	Refracts light that passes through it. Muscles can change the shape of the lens so it can refract light by different amounts (depending on how far away an object is). The more a lens is curved, the more light will refract.
Iris	Coloured part of the eye around the pupil. Light does not pass through the iris.
Pupil	Dark area in the middle of the eye. Light passes through the pupil. The eye has muscles that can open or close the iris. When it is very bright, the iris will be mostly closed and only a small part of the pupil will be seen. This is to protect the retina from damage. When it is dark, the opposite happens. The iris will be mostly open to allow more light to reach the retina.
Nerve	The nerve carries the signal from the retina to the brain.

Q1. The following statements are either true or false. State which are true and which are false.

a) A lens that is wider in the middle than at the edges is called a convex lens.

....

b) The human eye contains a convex lens.

....

c) The cornea contains cells that can detect light and colour.

....

d) The iris is the coloured part of the eye.

....

Q2. State three uses of convex lenses.

....

....

....

Q3. Complete the ray diagram to the right by showing the path of the rays of light from the lens to the focal point.

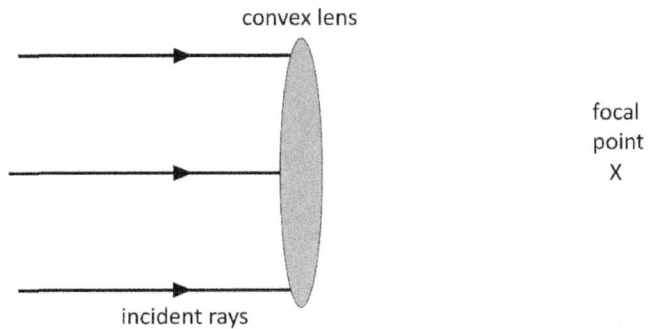

Q4. Describe how convex lenses bring rays of light together at a focal point.

....

....

Q5. Describe why the pupil appears larger on someone when it is dark, and smaller when it is very bright.

....

....

Q6. Using the diagram below, describe why the focal length (the distance from the lens to the focal point) of lens a) is more than that of lens b).

....

....

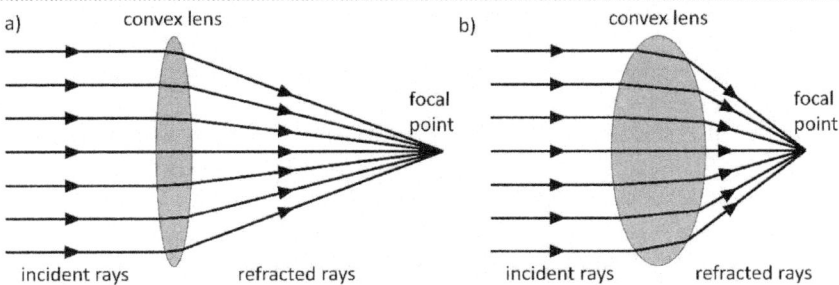

Cameras

A **pinhole camera** is a simple way of making an image of an object.

It consists of a box, with a small hole in one end and a "screen" at another. The screen should be made of a thin and **translucent** material like tracing paper. A translucent material is one that allows for some light to pass through it.

A diagram of a pinhole camera is below. Light rays are shown from the top and bottom of an object, but they come from all parts of the object.

Because the light rays from the top of the object are travelling at a different angle to the rays from the bottom of the object, the image is **inverted**. This means the image is upside down.

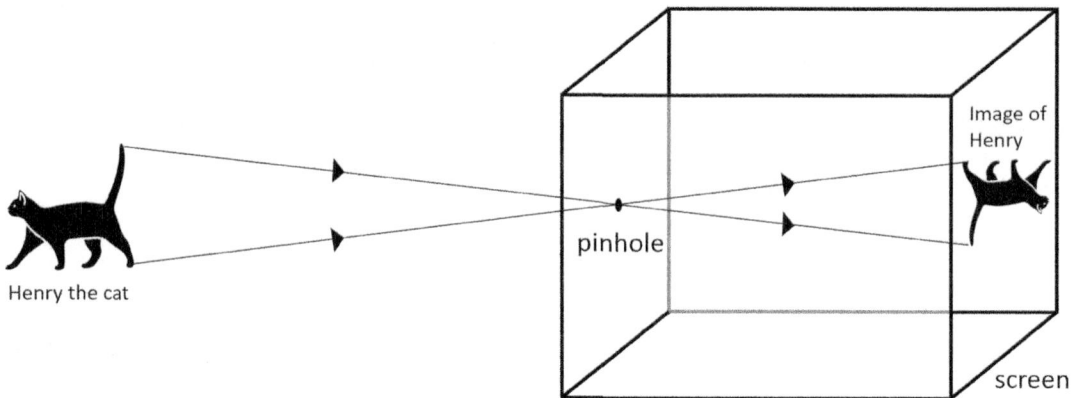

You can make a pinhole yourself at home by using a shoe box and some tracing paper.

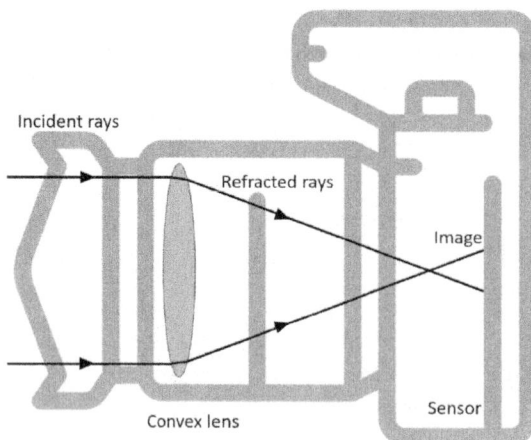

A more modern camera is shown in the diagram to the left.

Like the human eye, it contains a **convex lens**. The convex lens refracts light to a focus.

The camera also has a part of it that is sensitive to light. Instead of being called the retina (as it is in the eye), it is a sensor.

Even much smaller cameras (like the ones in phones) still contain lenses and sensors.

Q1. Describe what an object being translucent means.

....

....

Q2. Describe what an image being "inverted" means.

....

....

Q3. The following statements are either true or false. State which are true and which are false.

a) Both the human eye and a camera contain a convex lens.

....

b) The human eye contains a retina, while the equivalent for a camera is a sensor.

....

c) A pinhole camera contains a convex lens.

....

d) Images formed by a pinhole camera are always the same way up as the object.

....

Q4. Describe what refraction is and how a convex lens refracts light to a focus.

....

....

....

....

Q5. Complete the ray diagram below by showing the path of the rays of light from the lens to the focal point.

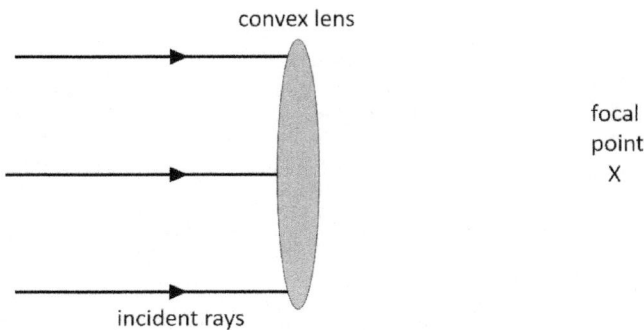

convex lens

focal
point
X

incident rays

Colours in light

White light is made from different individual colours. We know this because when we pass white light through a prism, the light is split up into seven different colours called a **spectrum**. This splitting of the colours is called **dispersion**. Dispersion is what causes **rainbows**.

The order of the colours (from longest to shortest wavelength) is:

Red   ↑ Longest wavelength
Orange
Yellow
Green
Blue
Indigo
Violet   Shortest wavelength

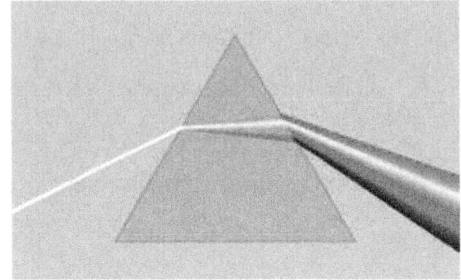

Commonly, people use ROY G. BIV to remember this order. Dispersion happens because the different colours of light experience a different **refractive index** and so **refract** by different amounts.

Violet refracts most as violet experiences the highest refractive index. You can remember this with the phrase "violet bends most violently". Red refracts least as red experiences the lowest refractive index.

A **filter** only allows one colour of light to be transmitted through it. Other colours are absorbed by the filter. The diagram below shows a red filter only letting red light go through it, a green filter only letting green light through it and a violet filter only letting violet light through it.

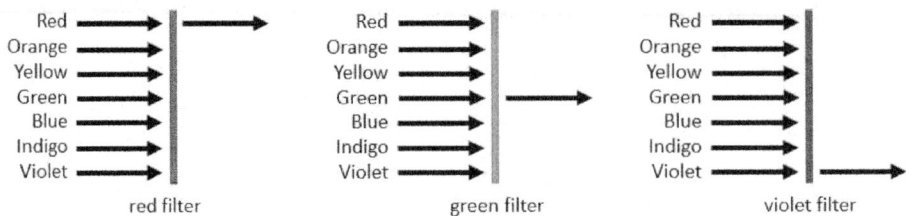

red filter   green filter   violet filter

In a similar way, different objects look coloured because of the light they reflect. A green object looks green because it reflects only green light into our eyes. A red object looks red because it reflects red light into our eyes. A white object reflects all seven colours of light in the spectrum.

Q1. The following statements are either true or false. State which are true and which are false.

a) All colours of light experience the same refractive index when going into a prism.

b) Dispersion is caused by refraction.

c) Dispersion is what causes rainbows.

d) Red light refracts most in a prism.

e) Of all the colours, red light has the longest wavelength.

Q2. Describe why dispersion happens.

Q3. State the order of colours in visible light, giving the order from longest to shortest wavelength.

Q4. State what colour of light is transmitted through an orange filter.

Q5. Describe why a blue object looks blue.

Q6. White light is passed through a yellow filter.

a) State what colour is transmitted through the yellow filter.

b) The light from this filter is then shone onto a blue object. Describe why the object looks black.

Electricity and

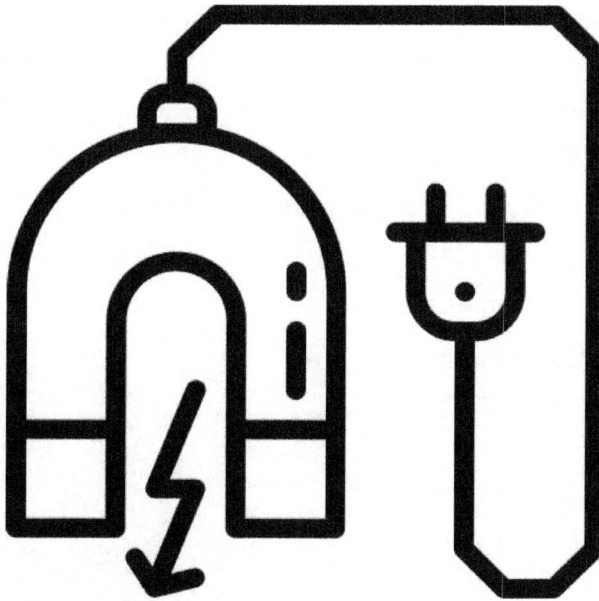

electromagnetism

Introduction to static electricity

All matter is made of **atoms** and **molecules**. In the centre of every atom is the **nucleus**. The nucleus is made of **protons** and **neutrons**. **Electrons** orbit around the nucleus.

Protons are positively charged, while electrons are negatively charged. Neutrons are **neutral** and so have no charge.

Atoms are neutral as they have equal numbers of protons and electrons. If an atom loses an electron then it becomes positively charged. We call an atom that has lost an electron an **ion** and call the process of an atom losing or gaining electrons **ionisation**.

Objects gain a static charge when one object rubs against another. The **friction** between these objects causes one to lose electrons and one to gain electrons.

Objects with different charges exert **electrostatic** forces on each other. This force is **non-contact**.

Like charges repel, unlike charges attract.

If somebody rubs a balloon against their hair, the friction transfers electrons from their hair onto the balloon.

If the balloon is removed from their hair, then the balloon will attract the hair. This is because the balloon and the hair have opposite charges.

Similarly, if two negatively charged balloons are placed next to each other then they will repel each other. This is because they have the same charge.

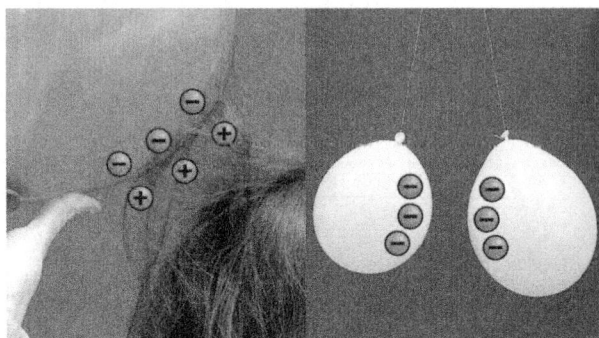

MikeRun, CC BY-SA 4.0 <https://creativecommons.org/licenses/by-sa/4.0>, via Wikimedia Commons

A Van de Graaff generator works in a similar way and very large charges can build up.

If somebody touches the surface of a Van de Graaff (while insulated from the floor) then the person gains a charge. This includes all of their hairs having the same charge. Because all of their hairs have the same charge, they repel each other and spread out.

Biswarup Ganguly, CC BY 3.0 <https://creativecommons.org/licenses/by/3.0>, via Wikimedia Commons

Q1. State the two particles that make up the nucleus.

....

Q2. State the name of the particle that orbits around the nucleus. State what charge it has.

....

Q3. State whether electrostatic forces are contact or non-contact. Explain what this means.

....

Q4. State the name of an atom that has lost or gained an electron.

....

Q5. Explain why atoms usually have no overall charge.

....

Q6. Describe how an object gains a static charge.

....

Q7. The following statements are either true or false. State which are true and which are false.

    a)   A positive charge attracts a negative charge.

....

    b)   A negative charge attracts a negative charge.

....

    c)   For an object to become charged, protons are transferred from one object to another.

....

Q8. A balloon is rubbed against someone's jumper. The balloon becomes negatively charged. Describe how the balloon becomes negatively charged. Include in your answer what charge the jumper will become.

....

....

....

Q9. Someone drags their feet while walking across a carpet. Describe why they might get an electric shock if they touch a metal door handle.

....

....

....

Electric field lines

Electrostatic forces are **non-contact**.

A **contact force** is one that acts when two objects are physically touching each other. Conversely, a **non-contact** force acts between objects that are not touching each other.

Non-contact forces are caused by a **field**. A charged object creates an electric field. The electric field lines for a positive and negative charge are shown in the image to the right.

Electric field lines point away from a positive charge and towards a negative charge.

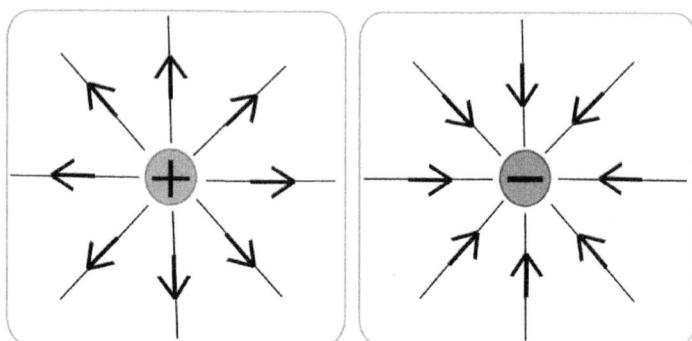

Nein Arimasen, CC BY-SA 3.0 <http://creativecommons.org/licenses/by-sa/3.0/>, via Wikimedia Commons

The electric field lines represent the direction of force that a nearby positive charge would experience (and the opposite to the direction of force on a nearby negative charge).

This is because **like charges repel and opposite charges attract**.

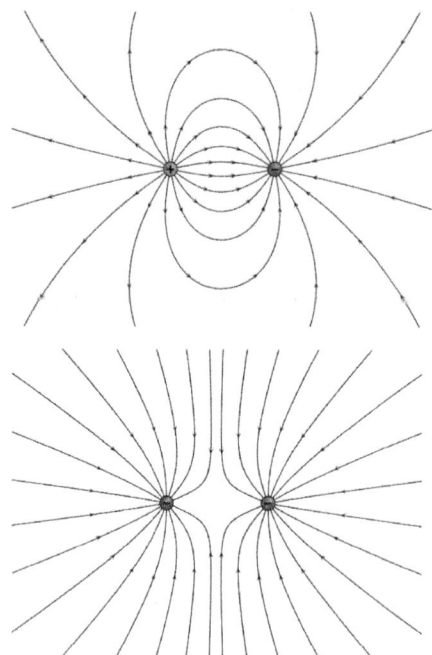

The closer together the field lines, the stronger the electric field. In the diagram above, the further you go away from each charge the weaker the field becomes. We know this because the field lines are further apart.

The top diagram to the left shows the electric field lines when a positive charge is near a negative charge.

The second diagram to the left shows the electric field lines when two negative charges are near each other. If there were two positive charges near each other the pattern would be identical but with the arrows pointing in the opposite direction (away from both positive charges).

In all cases, the electric field lines point away from positive charges and towards negative charges.

Geek3, CC BY-SA 3.0 <https://creativecommons.org/licenses/by-sa/3.0>, via Wikimedia Commons

Q1. State the direction that electric field lines point.

....

Q2. State the difference between a contact force and a non-contact force.

....

....

Q3. State whether electrostatic forces are contact or non-contact.

....

Q4. State whether like charges repel or attract.

....

Q5. In the space below, sketch the pattern of electric field lines around

    a) A positive charge.
    b) A negative charge.

Q6. State what the direction of the electric field lines represent.

....

Q7. State what the happens to the strength of the electric field as you go further from a charge.

....

Q8. In the space below, sketch the pattern of electric field lines around two positive charges that are near each other.

Circuit symbols

We use **circuit diagrams** to represent electrical circuits. We generally draw circuit diagrams in pencil and use a ruler to draw any connecting wires. **Circuit symbols** are used to represent different electrical components. A list of these circuit symbols are below:

A **connecting wire**. These are used to connect different parts of a circuit together.

A **cell** – provides **potential difference** to the circuit.

A **battery** – made of more than one cell.

A **lamp** – produces light.

A **resistor** – limits the amount of current in the circuit and is used to vary potential differences.

An o**pen switch**. When a switch is open that part of the circuit is **incomplete**. Current cannot flow through an incomplete circuit.

A **closed switch**. When a switch is closed that part of the circuit is **complete**. Current can flow through a complete circuit.

An **ammeter** – measures the **current** in a circuit. Goes in series in the part of the circuit where you want to measure the current.

A **voltmeter** – measures the potential difference between two parts of a circuit. Goes in parallel around the component that you want to measure the potential difference across.

The diagrams below show a **series** circuit (on the left) and a **parallel** circuit (on the right). Note how the connecting wires are all straight lines. A series circuit is one where there's only one path for the current to flow. A parallel circuit has more than one path.

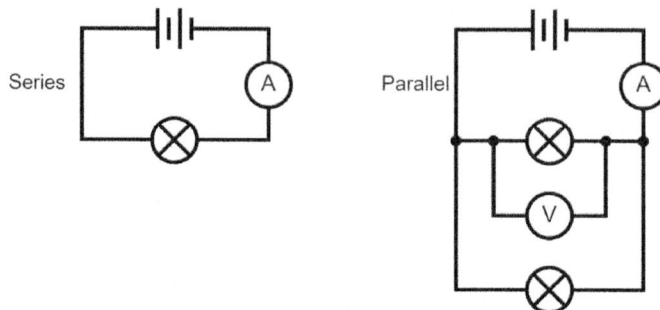

Q1. State the purpose of an ammeter.

....

Q2. Describe the difference between a series and a parallel circuit.

....

....

Q3. State the difference between a cell and a battery.

....

Q4. The following statements are either true or false. State which are true and which are false.

    a) Current can flow through an incomplete circuit.

....

    b) Voltmeters go in series with the component you want to measure the potential difference across.

....

Q5. In the space below, draw a series circuit that contains a battery, an open switch and a lamp.

Q6. In the space below, draw a series circuit that contains a cell, an ammeter, a resistor and a lamp. Also include a voltmeter in parallel around the lamp.

Q7. In the space below, draw a circuit that contains a battery and three lamps in parallel. On each path, include a switch so that each lamp can be switched on and off independently.

Current

Current flows through an electric circuit. Current is equal to how much **charge** is flowing past a point in the circuit every second. A **complete circuit** is needed for current to flow.

Current is measured in units of **amps** (A). An **ammeter** is used to measure the current at a point in the circuit. The circuit symbol for an ammeter is a circle with an "A" in it.

The charged particles that flow through a circuit are **electrons**. Electrons are **negatively charged** particles.

A **series** circuit only has one path for the current to flow. Therefore, **current is the same everywhere in a series circuit.**

The diagram to the right shows a series circuit with one lamp. The current is 2 A at each point in the circuit.

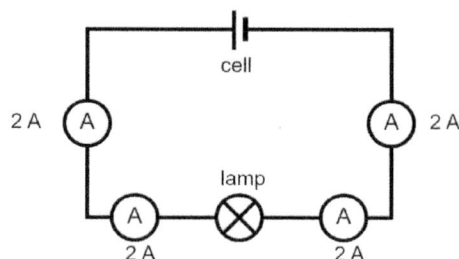

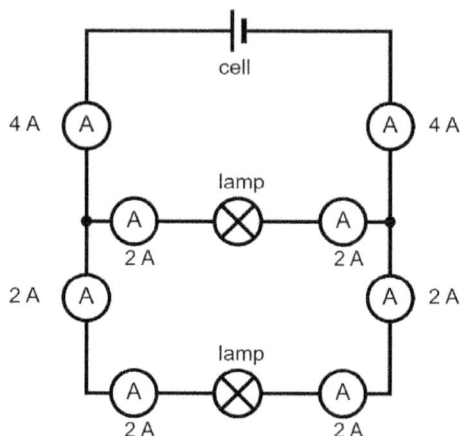

A **parallel** circuit has more than one path for the current to flow. The total current going into a **junction** (that is, where a wire splits or combines) is equal to the total current going out of a junction.

The circuit to the left shows a parallel circuit with each path having an identical lamp. Each branch has the same 2 A of current as before. Before and after each junction, though, the current is 4 A. **Each path draws additional current from the cell.**

To the right is a more complicated circuit diagram. All of the lamps are identical, so there is more **resistance** on one path than the other. The upper path has the same 2 A of current, but the lower path has twice the resistance (because there are two lamps) and so has half the current (at 1 A).

The overall current drawn from the battery is 3 A. **The higher the resistance in a path, the lower the current.**

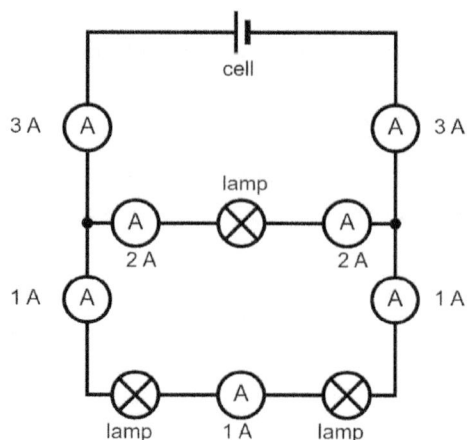

66

Q1. The following statements are either true or false. State which are true and which are false.

a) Current is equal to how much charge is flowing past a point in the circuit every second.

....

b) Protons are charged particles that flow through a circuit.

....

c) Current can flow through an incomplete circuit.

....

d) In a series circuit, current is different at different points.

....

Q2. State what we use to measure current in a circuit.

....

Q3. State the units of current.

....

Q4. In the space below, draw the circuit symbols for a cell, a lamp and an ammeter.

Q5. For each of the circuits below:

a) Circle whether the circuit is series or parallel.
b) For any ammeters that do not have a current written by them, write the missing current.

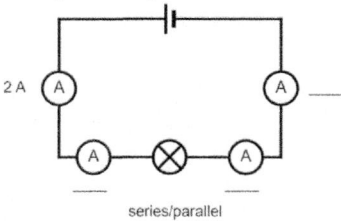

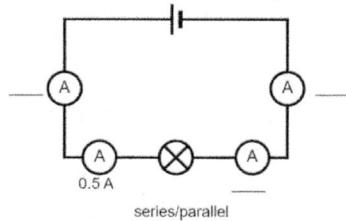

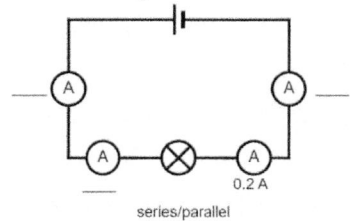

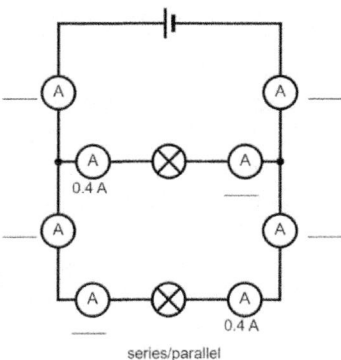

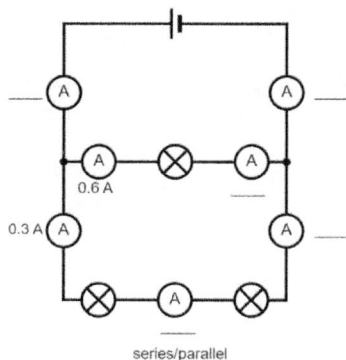

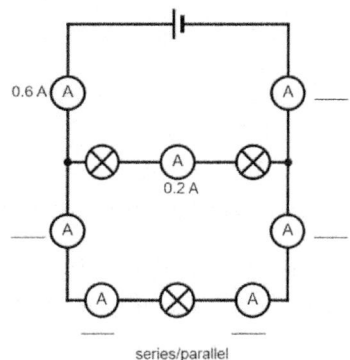

67

Potential difference

A battery or power supply gives each charge in an electrical circuit **energy**. Electrical components like lamps or resistors use this energy (which gets transferred into different energy stores). **Potential difference** is a measure of the difference in energy that charges have between each two points in a circuit.

Potential difference (commonly referred to as voltage) has units of **volts** (V) and is measured by a **voltmeter** which goes in **parallel** across the component you're measuring the potential difference across. The circuit symbol for a voltmeter is a circle with a "V" in it.

A circuit only experiences a drop in potential difference when the current goes through an electrical component. Therefore, **potential difference across each parallel branch is the same.**

The diagram to the right shows a cell that produces a potential difference of 10 V across it. The two resistors both have 10 V across them.

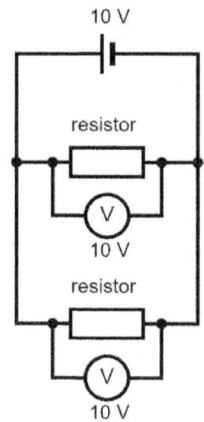

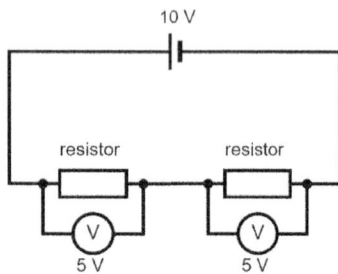

In a series circuit, potential difference is split across all components.

In the series circuit to the left, there are two identical resistors. Both resistors have a potential difference of 5 V across them (equal to half the potential difference across the cell).

The circuit diagram to the right is slightly more complicated. The total potential difference across each parallel path is 10 V. However, the lower path has two bulbs and so they each have 5 V across them.

Note how the top lamp is brightest. This is because it has a higher potential difference across it.

Lamps in parallel circuits have two main advantages:

- Each lamp receives the full potential difference and so is brighter.
- If there was a switch on each path, each lamp could be turned on and off independently. Remember that a circuit needs to be **complete** for a current to flow.

Lamps also have a **rating**. The lamp rating is the maximum potential difference that is safe to put across a lamp without it breaking.

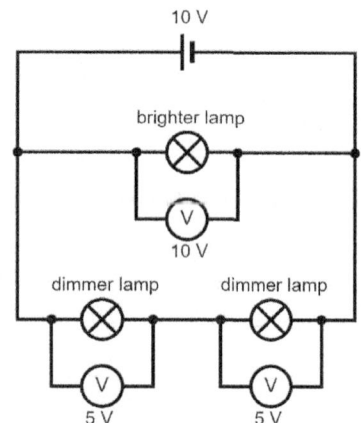

Q1. The following statements are either true or false. State which are true and which are false.

a) The potential difference across each parallel path is always the same.

....

b) In a series circuit, potential difference is the same everywhere.

....

c) The higher the potential difference across a lamp, the brighter the lamp.

....

d) The lamp rating is the potential difference the lamp turns on at.

....

e) Voltmeters go in series in a circuit.

....

Q2. State an advantage of having lamps in a parallel circuit.

....

Q3. In the space below, draw the circuit symbols for a resistor and a voltmeter.

Q4. Each of the circuits below have some voltmeters that do not have a potential difference written by them. Fill in the missing potential differences.

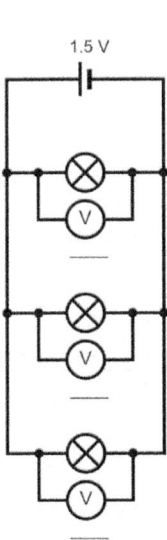

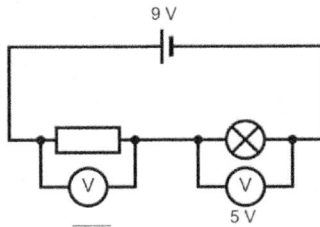

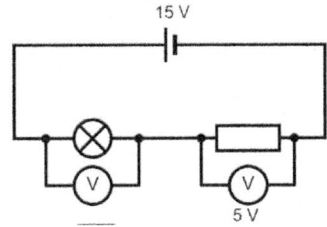

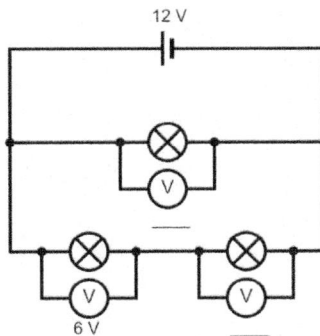

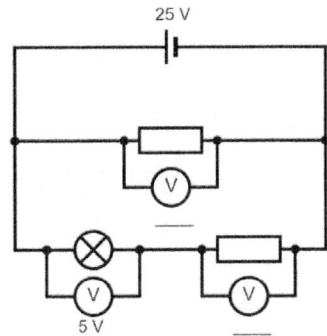

Resistance

Resistance is a measure of how hard it is for current to flow through an electrical component. Resistance is measured in **Ohms (Ω)**.

Electrical **conductors** (like metals) have a low resistance, while **insulators** (like plastic) have a high resistance.

There is an equation that relates potential difference, current and resistance:

Potential difference = Current × Resistance   or in symbols   **V = I × R**

Remember that potential difference has units of volts (V) and current has units of amps (A).

We can also rearrange this equation to give:

Resistance = Potential difference ÷ Current   or in symbols   **R = V ÷ I**

In words, **resistance is the ratio of potential difference to current**.

Example question 1:

A lamp has a resistance of 20 Ω and a current of 0.5 A flowing through it. Calculate the potential difference across the lamp.

Step 1. Write down equation: **V = I × R**

Step 2. Insert variables into equation: **= 0.5 × 20**

Step 3. Calculate answer. Remember units: **= 10 V**

Example question 2:

Using the information in the circuit diagram to the right, calculate the resistance of the resistor.

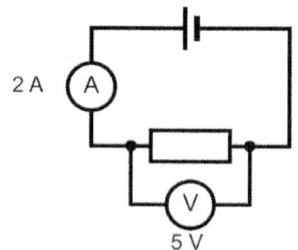

2 A

5 V

Step 1. Write down equation: **R = V ÷ I**

Step 2. Insert variables into equation: **R = 5 ÷ 2**

Step 3. Calculate answer. Remember units: **= 2.5 Ω**

Sometimes resistance is given in units of **kiloohms (kΩ)**. One kiloohm is equal to one thousand Ohms. To convert from kiloohms to Ohms you need to multiply the number of kilowatts by one thousand: **kΩ × 1000 → Ω**. You need to convert to Ohms for calculations.

Q1. State the equation that links potential difference, current and resistance.

....

Q2. State the unit of resistance.

....

Q3. Describe the difference between an electrical conductor and an insulator.

....

Q4. A lamp has a resistance of 15 Ω and a current of 2.0 A flowing through it. Calculate the potential difference across the lamp.

$$V = I \times R$$

$$= 2.0 \text{ A} \times 15 \text{ Ω}$$

$$= \text{_____} \text{ V}$$

Q5. A resistor has a resistance of 500 Ω and a current of 0.10 A flowing through it. Calculate the potential difference across the resistor.

$$V = I \times R$$

$$= \text{\_\_\_\_ \_\_} \times \text{\_\_\_\_ \_\_}$$

$$= \text{_____} \text{ V}$$

Q6. Using the information in the diagram to the right, calculate the resistance of the lamp.

$$R = V \div I$$

$$= \text{\_\_\_\_ \_\_} \div \text{\_\_\_\_ \_\_}$$

$$= \text{_____} \text{ Ω}$$

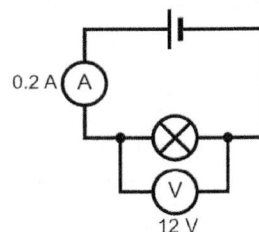

0.2 A (A)

12 V

Q7. A resistor has a resistance of 100 Ω and a current of 0.8 A flowing through it. Calculate the potential difference across the resistor.

....

Q8. A light dependent resistor (LDR) has a potential difference of 6 V across it and a current of 0.02 A flowing through it. Calculate the resistance of the LDR.

....

Q9. A thermistor has a resistance of 1.5 kΩ and a current of 0.5 A flowing through it. Calculate the potential difference across the thermistor.

....

Q10. A resistor has a resistance of 2.0 kΩ and a potential difference of 10 V across it. Calculate the current flowing through the resistor.

....

Introduction to magnetism

Magnetism is a **non-contact force**.

A **contact force** is one that acts when two objects are physically touching each other. Conversely, a **non-contact** force acts between objects that are not touching each other.

Non-contact forces are caused by a **field**. The magnetic field lines for a bar magnet are shown in the diagram to the right.

The bar magnet consists of a **north** pole and a **south** pole. The magnetic field lines point away from the North pole and towards the South pole. The field lines give the direction of force on the North pole of another magnet.

Like poles repel. Unlike poles attract.

The diagram also shows the magnetic field is

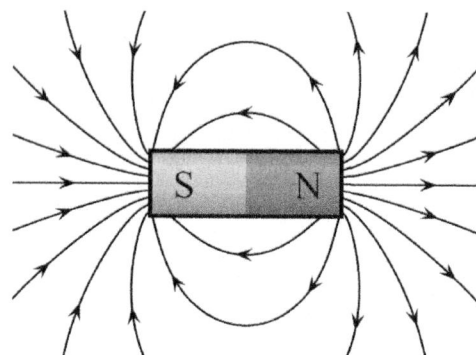

By Geek3 - Own work, CC BY-SA 3.0, https://commons.wikimedia.org/w/index.php?curid=10587 119

stronger near the ends (**poles**) of the bar magnet. We can tell this because the magnetic field lines are closer together.

A **permanent magnet** (like a bar magnet) produces its own magnetic field. There are three metals that become magnetic when placed in a magnetic field. These magnetic metals are **iron, nickel and cobalt**. Steel is also a magnetic metal as it contains iron. Metals other than these are not magnetic.

The magnetic metals are attracted by permanent magnets, but never repelled.

A permanent magnet can be **demagnetised** by heating it, hitting it with a hammer or by placing it in a reversed magnetic field.

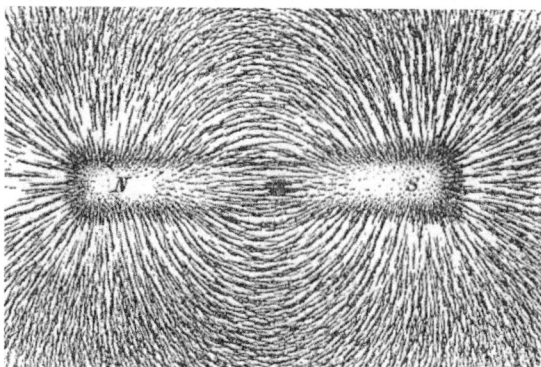

Newton Henry Black, Harvey N. Davis (1913) Practical Physics, The MacMillan Co., USA, p. 242, fig. 200, Public Domain, https://commons.wikimedia.org/w/index.php?curid=73846

We can visualise the magnetic field around a bar magnet by using **iron filings**. A bar magnet can be put under a piece of paper, with iron filings then sprinkled on top of the paper.

The iron filings arrange themselves in the shape of the field and are most attracted to the regions with the strongest field (the poles). This is shown in the diagram to the left.

Q1. State the direction that magnetic lines point.

....

Q2. State the difference between a contact force and a non-contact force.

....

....

Q3. State whether magnetism is a contact or non-contact force.

....

Q4. In the space below, sketch the magnetic field lines around a bar magnet.

Q5. State the three magnetic metals.

....

Q6. The following statements are either true or false. State which are true and which are false.

    a) Cobalt is attracted to a bar magnet.

....

    b) A north pole repels another north pole.

....

    c) Copper is attracted to a bar magnet.

....

    d) A north pole attracts a south pole.

....

    e) The closer together the magnetic field lines, the stronger the field.

....

    f) Iron is repelled by a bar magnet.

....

    g) Magnetic field lines point away from a south pole and towards a north pole.

....

Plotting magnetic fields

We already know that we can use **iron filings** to show the magnetic field around a bar magnet. Iron filings don't show the direction of the field, though. If we want to show the direction of a magnetic field then we need to use **plotting compasses**.

A plotting compass is a **small bar magnet** that is free to rotate. The north pole of the small bar magnet in the compass will always point towards magnetic south. The compass points towards magnetic south.

To show the direction of the field, we can place a bar magnet on a piece of paper and place a plotting around near one of its poles. The direction of the compass can then be marked and the compass moved to various other positions. The arrows can then be joined up to show the overall field shape.

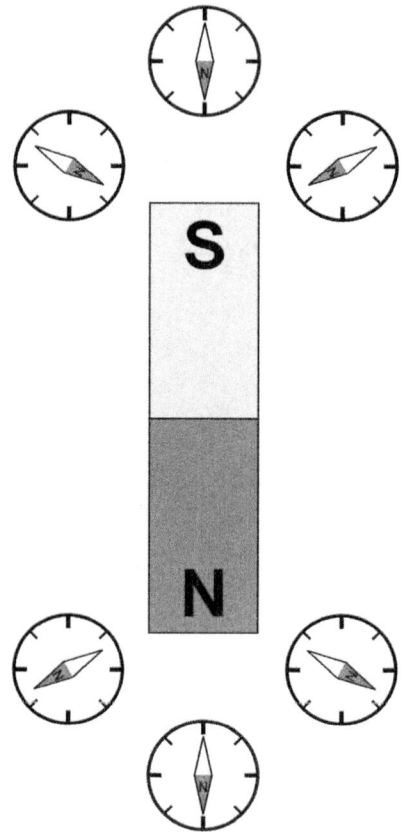

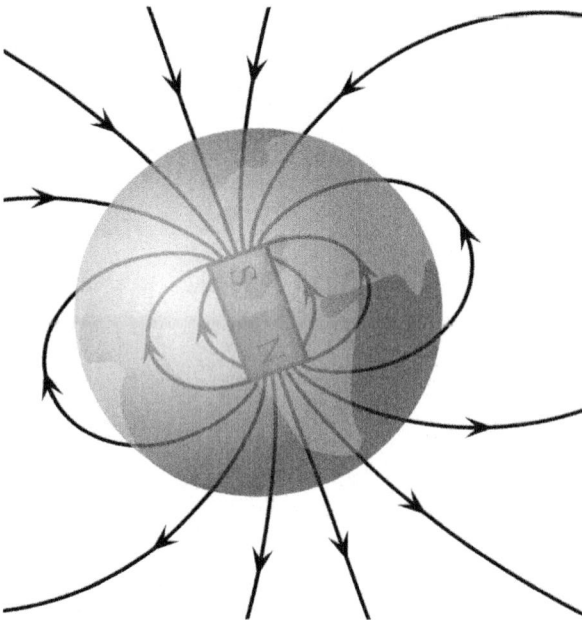

Compasses are also used to help navigate. The Earth's outer core is made of molten iron and nickel and so it has its own magnetic field, in the same shape as that of a bar magnet.

Confusingly, the geographic North pole of the Earth is near (but not precisely at) its magnetic south pole.

A compass always points to Earth's magnetic south.

Q1. The following statements are either true or false. State which are true and which are false.

a) A compass points towards **Earth's** magnetic north.

....

b) A compass can be used for navigation.

....

c) The geographic North pole of Earth is near its magnetic south pole.

....

Q2. State what a compass is made of.

....

Q3. State what the outer core of the Earth is made of.

....

Q4. Your answer to question 3 should contain two of the three magnetic metals. State the other magnetic metal.

....

Q5. When visualising the magnetic field around a magnet, state a benefit of using a compass over iron filings.

....

Q6. Electronic devices (like a mobile phone) produce a magnetic field. Describe why a compass should not be used near an electronic device.

....

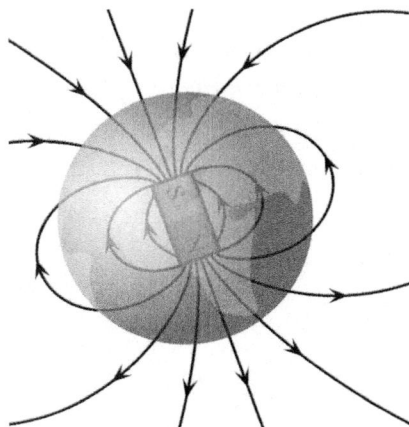

Q7. State where the magnetic field is strongest on the Earth. Explain, using the diagram to the left, how we know this.

....

....

Q8. Explain if we would be able to use compasses to navigate if the Earth didn't have a magnetic field.

....

....

VFPt Earths Magnetic Field Confusion.svg:
Geek3 / derivative work: MikeRun, CC BY-SA 3.0
<https://creativecommons.org/licenses/by-
sa/3.0>, via Wikimedia Commons

Electromagnetism

Any time a **current** flows through a wire, a magnetic field is formed around the wire. This is called an **electromagnet**. The magnetic field can be made stronger by increasing the current.

The magnetic field is strongest near to the wire and gets weaker further away.

If the current stops flowing, then the magnetic field also stops.

The field around a current carrying wire is in concentric circles around the wire. The circles are closer together closer to the wire. This shows the magnetic field is strongest nearer the wire. We can see what direction the magnetic field goes in by using the **right hand rule**.

Here, you point the thumb on your right hand along the direction of current. The direction that your fingers point give the direction of the magnetic field. This is shown in the diagram to the right. The current is labelled *I*, and the magnetic field is labelled *B*.

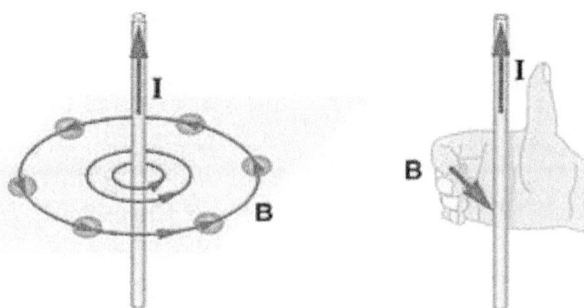

OpenStax, CC BY 4.0 <https://creativecommons.org/licenses/by/4.0>, via Wikimedia Commons

We could also show the direction of the field by using **plotting compasses** in the same way that we used them to show the shape of a magnetic field around a bar magnet.

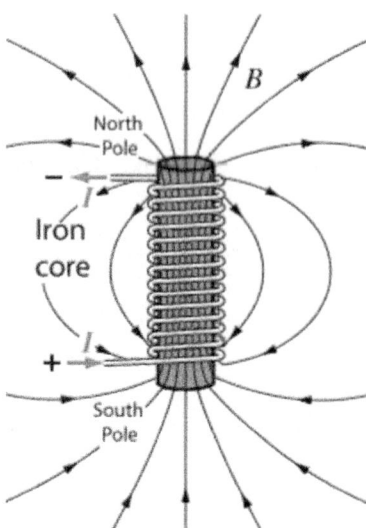

A coil of wire is called a **solenoid**. A solenoid creates a magnetic field in the same pattern as a bar magnet. The magnetic field is strongest inside a solenoid. There are three ways to increase the strength of the field produced by a solenoid:

1. Increase the number of turns in the coil.
2. Increase the current.
3. Add an **iron core**.

Iron is an example of a **soft** magnetic material. A soft magnetic material can be easily magnetised and demagnetised. This is an advantage as we want electromagnets to be able to easily turn their magnetism on and off. A **hard** magnetic material is difficult to magnetise and demagnetise. **A hard material shouldn't be used in the core of a solenoid as it would retain some magnetism.**

P.Sumanth Naik, CC BY-SA 3.0 <https://creativecommons.org/licenses/by-sa/3.0>, via Wikimedia Commons

Q1. State what has to flow through a wire to create an electromagnet.

....

Q2. Describe what a solenoid is.

....

Q3. State where the magnetic field produced by a solenoid is strongest.

....

Q4. State three ways of making the magnetic field around a solenoid stronger.

....

....

....

Q5. Describe the difference between a soft magnetic material and a hard magnetic material.

....

....

Q6. State one example of a soft magnetic material.

....

Q7. Describe why hard magnetic materials are not placed in a solenoid.

....

....

Q8. State what happens to the strength of the magnetic field as you go further from a current carrying wire.

....

Q9. Describe the shape of a magnetic field around a current carrying wire.

....

Q10. State what the direction of the thumb represents in the right hand rule.

....

Q11. State what the direction of the fingers represent in the right hand rule.

....

Q12. Other than using the right hand rule, state how we could show the direction of a field around a current carrying wire.

....

Electric motors

The construction of an electric motor is quite simple, it is made of a coil of wire inside a magnetic field. The magnetic field is produced by two permanent magnets.

In the diagram to the right, a battery supplies a **current** to a coil of wire (labelled armature). When a current flows through a wire, it creates a magnetic field. The magnetic field is labelled "B", and the field lines point away from a north pole towards a south pole.

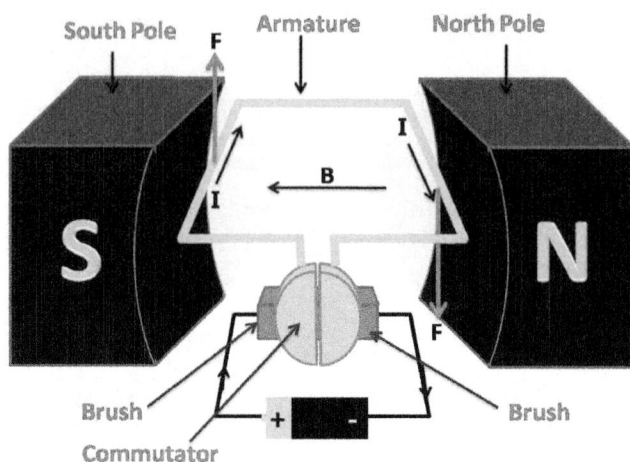

K.Venkataramana, CC BY-SA 4.0 <https://creativecommons.org/licenses/by-sa/4.0>, via Wikimedia Commons

This magnetic field interacts with the permanent magnetic field that surrounds the coil. This interaction produces a **force**.

A coil of wire is used, as the more turns in the coil the greater the strength of the overall magnetic field produced and the greater the force on the coil.

On the left side of the coil in the diagram this interaction of magnetic fields leads to an upwards force. As the current (labelled I) goes around the coil, though, it changes direction. There is therefore a downwards force on the right side of the coil in the diagram. These forces lead to a rotation of the coil.

However, if the coil rotates by 180° then the direction of those forces would reverse. To counter this a **split ring commutator** is used. A split ring commutator reverses the direction of current every half turn. This ensures the motor continues to rotate in the same direction. The **brushes** (made of carbon) rub against the split ring commutator and allow it to rotate.

There are three main ways to make an electric motor rotate faster:

- Increase the current flowing through the coil.
- Increase the number of turns in the coil.
- Increase the strength of the magnetic field.

There are two ways of making an electric motor rotate in the opposite direction. You can either reverse the direction of the current or reverse the direction of the magnetic field produced by the permanent magnets.

Q1. The following statements are either true or false. State which are true and which are false.

   a) When a current flows through a wire, it creates a magnetic field.

   b) Magnetic field lines point away from a south pole towards a north pole.

Q2. State the components in an electric motor.

Q3. Explain why there is a force on the coil in an electric motor.

Q4. Describe the role of the split ring commutator in an electric motor.

Q5. State three ways of making an electric motor rotate faster.

Q6. State two ways of making an electric motor rotate in the opposite direction.

Q7. State what the brushes in an electric motor are made of.

Q8. The current supplied to an electric motor is switched off. Explain why the motor stops spinning.

Q9. The battery powering an electric motor has been used for a long time and the current supplied by the battery is starting to decrease. Explain what happens to the electric motor.

Speakers and microphones

A speaker is made from a coil of wire, a permanent magnet and a cone.

A **current** flows into the coil of wire. Any time a current flows through a wire, a **magnetic field** is formed around the wire.

This magnetic field interacts with the field caused by the permanent magnets. This causes a **force** which, in turn, causes the cone to move.

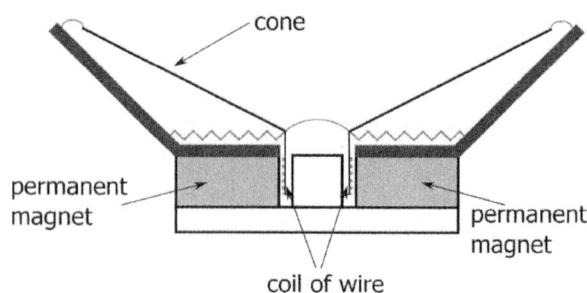

Adapted from: Harkonnen2 - Loudspeakerconstruction.png, CC BY-SA 3.0, https://commons.wikimedia.org/w/index.php?curid=9540717

If the current changes direction, then the magnetic field caused by the coil changes direction. This causes the force on the coil to be in the opposite direction to before.

A current that constantly changes direction is called an **alternating current**.

If the current constantly changes direction, then so does the direction of the force on the cone. The cone therefore vibrates back and forth, making a sound. The **vibration** of an object is what makes sound.

The **frequency** of the sound made is the same as the frequency of vibration. The faster the vibration of the cone, the higher the frequency of sound made.

There are three ways of making this sound louder:

- Increase the current flowing through the coil.
- Increase the number of turns in the coil.
- Increase the strength of the magnetic field caused by the permanent magnet.

A **microphone** is built in the same way as a speaker but works in the opposite way.

In a microphone, a sound wave comes onto the cone and causes it to vibrate. In a microphone, the cone is sometimes called a **diaphragm**.

This causes the coil of wire to vibrate and the coil moves within the magnetic field of the permanent magnet.

Any time a coil of wire experiences a change in magnetic field (as it would when it moves in a magnetic field) then it causes a current to flow in the coil.

This changing current in the coil could then be passed into a speaker for playing (or the pattern of the changing current could be saved to play later).

Q1. The following statements are either true or false. State which are true and which are false.

a) Any time a current passes through a wire, a magnetic field is formed around the wire.

....

b) A microphone contains a diaphragm which vibrates when sound reaches it.

....

c) An alternating current is one that always flows in the same direction.

....

d) If a coil moves in a magnetic field, a current is made.

....

e) If the current in the coil in a speaker is decreased, the sound made by the speaker is louder.

....

Q2. State the names of the three different parts of a speaker.

....

Q3. Describe what an alternating current is.

....

Q4. Describe how a speaker makes a sound.

....

....

....

....

Q5. State three ways of making a speaker make a louder sound.

....

....

....

Q6. Describe how a microphone works.

....

....

....

....

Matter

Particle model

All matter is made of **particles**. Depending on the substance, the particles could be **atoms** or **molecules**.

The three **states of matter** are **solid**, **liquid**, and **gas**. They all have different properties due to the arrangement and movement of their particles.

Solid

Solids have particles that are held tightly together. The particles are arranged in a regular pattern and **vibrate around fixed positions.** Solids have a definite shape and volume. Solids are **dense** and they **cannot be compressed** easily because the particles are already packed closely together. Solids have the least amount of energy.

Liquid

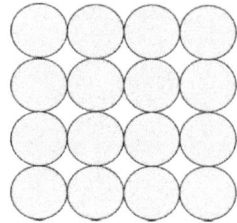

In a **liquid** the particles are held closely together but the particles can also move past each other. This means that a liquid has a changing shape and can **flow**. Liquids are **dense** and **cannot be compressed** easily (**hydraulics** make use of this). A liquid can change its shape but not its volume.

Gas

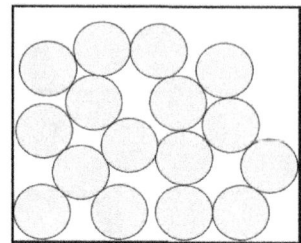

There are only **very weak forces** between **gas** particles, which are far apart. Because of this gases can be **compressed**, and so they have no fixed volume. The particles move around quickly in random directions, at a range of different speeds. They cause pressure when they collide with the walls of a container. Gases have a **low density** and they do not have a fixed shape or volume. Gases have the most energy. As you heat a gas, the particles move more quickly.

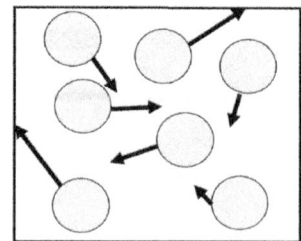

While solids are usually the most dense state of matter; water and ice are an exception. Water (a liquid) is more dense than ice (a solid). That's why ice cubes float in a drink.

Q1. In the spaces below, draw the particle arrangement for solids liquids and gases.

Solids	Liquids	Gases

Q2. Name the state of matter that can be compressed. ....

Q3. Name the state of matter that can change its shape but not its volume. ....

Q4. Name the state of matter that has no fixed volume. ....

Q5. Name the state of matter that has a low density. ....

Q6. Name the state of matter that has particles that vibrate around fixed positions. ....

Q7. Name the state of matter that is used in hydraulics. ....

Q8. Name the state of matter that has particles that flow but are still close together. ....

Q9. State what happens to the speed of gas particles when the temperature of a gas is increased.

....

Q10. Describe the movement of gas particles.

....

....

Q11. Describe how the particle arrangement changes as a material changes from a solid into a liquid.

....

....

....

....

Q12. Describe how the particle arrangement changes as a material changes from a liquid into a gas.

....

....

....

....

Q13. State the reason why ice cubes float in water.

....

State changes

As the temperature of particles changes, they **change state**. In the process of changing state, the overall number of particles stays the same. This means the mass before a state change is the same as the mass after a state change. This is called the **conservation of mass**. The different state changes are shown in the diagram below:

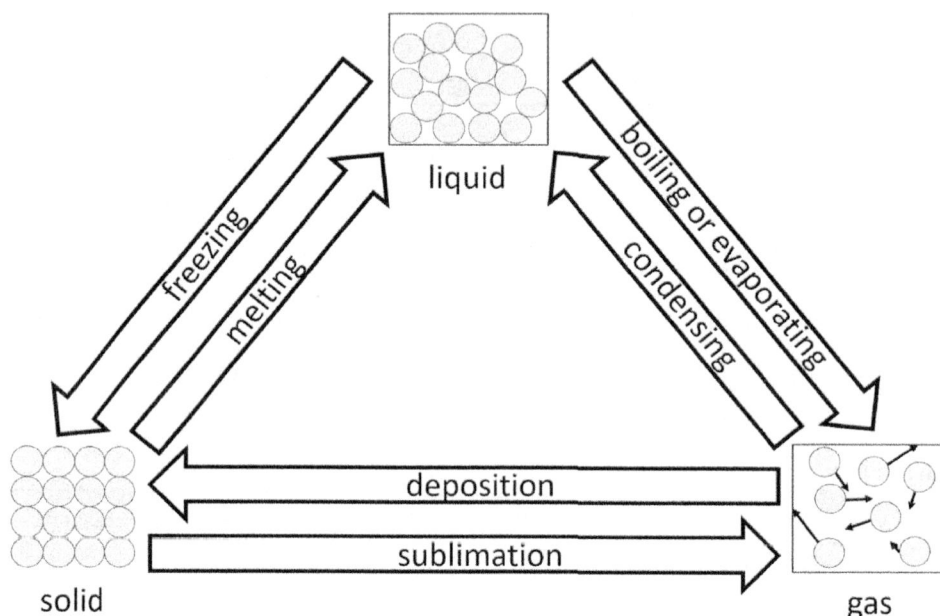

A **solid** has particles that are held together in a regular pattern. The particles vibrate around their fixed positions. As the solid is heated, these vibrations increase until it reaches its **melting point**. One example of a melting point is that of water at 0°C.

While the solid is melting, it stays at the same temperature. The particles start to be freed from their fixed positions until they are free to move past each other. Particles are still in contact. When the process of melting is complete, all the particles are in the **liquid** state.

If we continue heating the liquid, the particles again move more quickly. When the liquid reaches its **boiling point**, it starts boiling and turning into a **gas**. Here, the particles are moving quickly enough so they separate from one another. Particles in a gas are far apart and move around quickly in random directions. One example of a boiling point is that of water at 100°C.

If a gas is cooled to its boiling point, it **condenses** into a liquid. If a liquid is cooled to its melting point, it **freezes** to form a solid.

If cooled enough, gases can also undergo **deposition** so they are turned directly into a solid. If heated enough, solids can undergo **sublimation** so they are turned directly into a gas.

Q1. During a state change, mass is conserved. Describe what conservation of mass means.

....

....

Q2. Name the state change in going from solid to liquid. ....

Q3. Name the state change in going from gas to liquid. ....

Q4. Name the state change in going from liquid to gas. ....

Q5. Name the state change in going from gas to solid. ....

Q6. Name the state change in going from solid to gas. ....

Q7. Name the state change in going from liquid to solid. ....

Q8. State the melting point of water. ....

Q9. State the boiling point of water. ....

Q10. Describe the particle arrangement in a solid.

....

....

Q11. Describe the particle arrangement in a gas.

....

....

Q12. The following statements are either true or false. State which are true and which are false.

   a) As a solid melts, the temperature increases.

....

   b) As a gas is heated, the particles move more quickly.

....

   c) Regardless of temperature, particles in a solid vibrate the same amount.

....

   d) If particles in a liquid evaporate into a gas, the gas has less mass than the liquid.

....

Q13. Some water is at a temperature of −10°C. State which state of matter the water is in. Explain why.

....

Q14. Some water is at a temperature of 200°C. State which state of matter the water is in. Explain why.

....

Q15. Some water is at a temperature of 50°C. State which state of matter the water is in. Explain why.

....

Heating and cooling curves

The graph below shows the heating curve of a **pure** substance. A pure substance is made from only one element or compound. Note how the temperature of the substance remains constant during a state change.

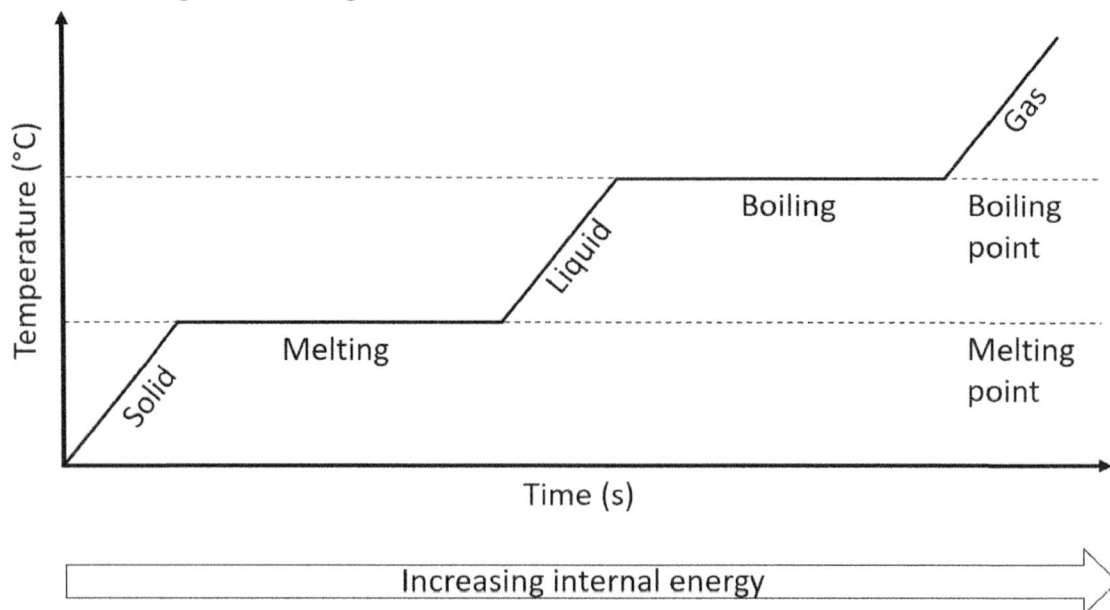

As thermal energy is transferred to the substance, the **internal energy** of the particles in the substance increases. The internal energy consists of the **kinetic energy** and **potential energy** stores of the particles.

While the substance is increasing in temperature, the kinetic energy store of the particles in the substance increases. As a solid increases in temperature, the vibrations of the particles in the solid increase.

Eventually, the solid start melting. During this time, some bonds are broken but the temperature remains constant. The potential energy store of the particles in the substance increases. The thermal energy supplied to the material is called "latent" here. Latent comes from the Latin for "hidden".

Similar happens with liquids and gases. As a liquid or gas increases in temperature, particles move more quickly and their kinetic energy store increases. As a liquid is boiled, bonds are broken and the potential energy store of particles increases.

An **impure** substance contains more than one element or compound. We could also say the substance contains **impurities**. For an impure substance, there is not a single temperature for melting and boiling. Instead, this happens over a range of temperatures.

Q1. The diagram below shows the cooling curve of a pure substance. Label the three states of matter that are missing from the diagram.

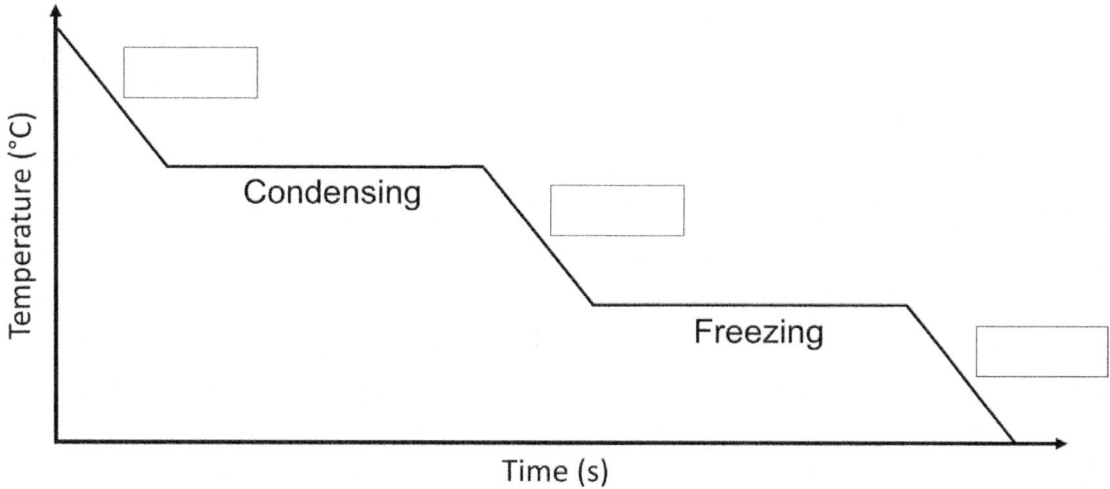

Q2. Describe what a pure substance is.

....

....

Q3. Describe what happens to the motion and kinetic energy of gas particles as they cool.

....

....

Q4. Describe what internal energy is.

....

....

Q5. Describe what an impure substance is.

....

....

Q6. Describe how the heating curve for an impure substance is different to that of a pure substance.

....

....

Q7. Describe why the temperature of a pure substance stays constant while it melts.

....

....

Q8. State what happens to the internal energy of a substance as it increases in temperature.

....

Pressure in gases

Particles in a gas move **in random directions** and at a range of different speeds.

We know this because of something called **Brownian motion**. In 1827, Robert Brown (which Brownian motion is named after) noticed that pollen particles moved around in a random way. Smoke particles move in a similar way in air. This is because of collisions with air particles that are moving in random directions and at a range of different speeds.

While the smoke particles are much larger than the air particles, the air particles are moving much faster and so they affect how the smoke particles move when they collide.

When a gas particle collides with a surface, **pressure** is exerted on that surface.

The reason balloons get bigger when you blow them up is because you are adding air into the balloon.

More air means **more particles** inside the balloon. In turn, this leads to **more collisions** between air particles and the walls of the balloon. More collisions cause a **higher force** on the walls, which then leads to a **higher pressure**. This makes the balloon **expand**.

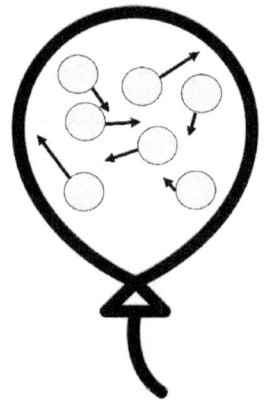

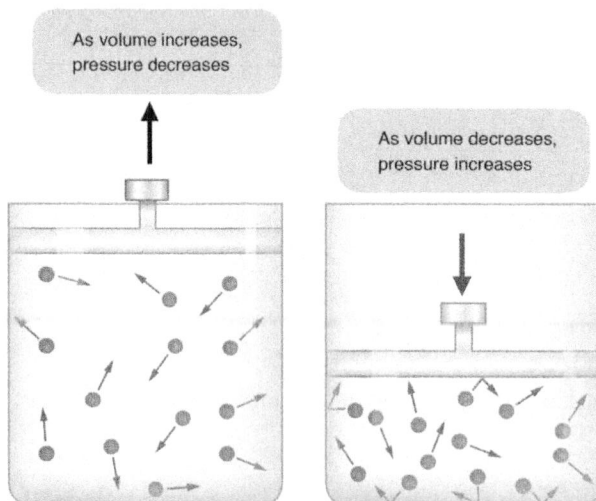

As volume increases, pressure decreases

As volume decreases, pressure increases

If we reduce the volume of a container, a similar thing happens. This is shown in the diagram to the left.

If the volume of a container is reduced, gas particles collide with the walls of the container more often.

This leads to a higher force on the walls of the container, and therefore a higher pressure.

OpenStax College, CC BY 3.0 <https://creativecommons.org/licenses/by/3.0>, via Wikimedia Commons

If we increase the temperature of a gas in a container, the **kinetic energy** and speed of the gas particles also increase. This also means the gas particles collide with the walls of the container more often (again leading to a higher force and a higher pressure on the walls of the container). This is why a balloon expands if we heat it.

Q1. Smoke particles are observed to move in a random way in air. State the name of this process and explain why this happens.

....

....

Q2. Air is being pumped into a balloon.

  a) State what happens to the number of air particles inside the balloon.

....

  b) State what happens to the number of collisions between the air particles and the walls of the balloon.

....

  c) State what happens to the force exerted by the air particles on the walls of the balloon.

....

  d) State what happens to the pressure inside the balloon.

....

  e) State what happens to the size of the balloon.

....

Q3. Some gas is inside a container. The volume of the container is slowly increased.

  a) State what happens to the force exerted by the air particles on the walls of the container.

....

  b) State what happens to the pressure inside the container.

....

Q4. State what happens to the average speed of gas particles as the temperature of the gas is increased.

....

Q5. Two containers have the same amount of gas particles inside them. Container A is smaller than container B. State and explain which container has the higher pressure.

....

....

Q6. Two containers have the same amount of gas particles inside them. Container A is at a lower temperature than container B. State and explain which container has the higher pressure.

....

....

Q7. A balloon is cooled. State and explain what happens to the size of the balloon.

....

....

Diffusion

Particles in liquids and gases move in a **random motion**. Particles in a liquid are in contact with each other and free to flow past each other. Particles in a gas are separate from one another and move quickly in random directions at a range of speeds. We also know that this causes **Brownian motion**.

Diffusion happens in fluids (liquids and gases). Diffusion is the movement of particles from a high concentration (of those particles) to a lower concentration.

The diagram below shows some purple dye being introduced to a glass of water. Because the water particles are moving in random directions, this leads to diffusion of the purple dye.

Immediately after the dye has been dropped it is at a high concentration in that area. Diffusion means that particles move from this high concentration to the surrounding areas (where there is a low concentration). Eventually the dye is evenly spread throughout the water.

BruceBlaus, CC BY 3.0, https://commons.wikimedia.org/w/index.php?curid=29452222

The diagram to the right also shows the initial and final stages in terms of particles. If we leave the water and dye for long enough then the dye particles are evenly distributed throughout the water.

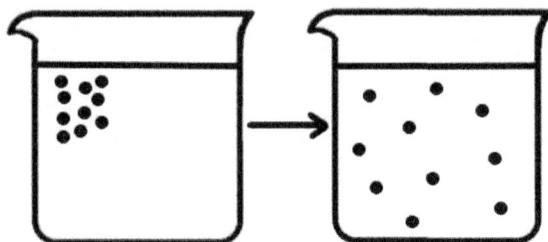

Christinelmiller, CC BY-SA 4.0
https://creativecommons.org/licenses/by-sa/4.0, via Wikimedia Commons

If we wanted to speed this process up, then we could heat the water. Particles move faster in a hotter liquid or gas. Therefore diffusion would also be faster. We could also speed up diffusion by stirring the liquid.

Q1. The following statements are either true or false. State which are true and which are false.

a) In diffusion, particles move from a low concentration to a high concentration.

....

b) Diffusion happens at the same rate, regardless of the temperature of the liquid.

....

c) Diffusion happens only in liquids.

....

d) Diffusion in a liquid can be sped up by stirring the liquid.

....

Q2. Describe how particles move in liquids.

....

....

Q3. Describe how particles move in gases.

....

....

Q4. Describe what diffusion is.

....

....

Q5. State what happens to the average speed of particles in a liquid as the temperature of the liquid is increased.

....

Q6. Two beakers are full of water. Some red dye is dropped in each. Beaker A contains water at 20 °C, Beaker B contains water at 50 °C. State and explain in which beaker diffusion will be fastest.

....

....

Q7. Some deodorant is sprayed in a room. Explain how the deodorant spreads throughout the room.

....

....

Q8. A fan is on in the same room. State what this would do to the rate of diffusion.

....

Density

Density is a measure of how much **mass** is in a given **volume**.

Low Density

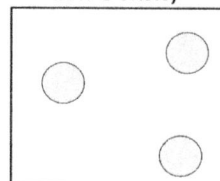

The diagram to the right shows three gases in the same volume. If we assume that each particle has the same mass, then the top gas must have the least density and the lowest gas must have the highest density.

The density of an object can be calculated using the equation:

Medium Density

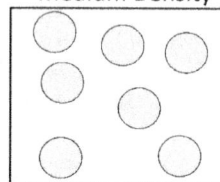

$$\text{Density} = \text{Mass} \div \text{Volume}$$

The **mass** of an object is the amount of matter it contains and is measured in **kilograms** (kg). The **volume** is the amount of space that an object takes up and is measured in **metres cubed** (m^3).

High Density

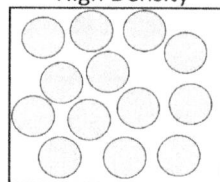

Density has units of **kilograms per metre cubed** (kg/m^3).

Example question 1: Some wood has a mass of 210 kg and a volume of 0.3 m^3. Calculate the density of the wood.

Step 1. Write down equation: **Density = Mass ÷ Volume**

Step 2. Insert variables into equation: **= 210 kg ÷ 0.3 m^3**

Step 3. Calculate answer. Remember units: **= 700 kg/m^3**

The density of water is equal to 1000 kg/m^3. Anything lower than this density will float on water. Therefore the wood that we calculated the density of in the example question will float on water.

Example question 2: The density of granite is 2700 kg/m^3. Some granite has a mass of 5400 kg, calculate the volume of the granite.

Step 1. Write down equation: **Density = Mass ÷ Volume**

Step 2. Insert variables into equation: **2700 kg/m^3 = 5400 kg ÷ Volume**

Step 3. Rearrange equation: **Volume = 5400 kg ÷ 2700 kg/m^3**

Step 3. Calculate answer. Remember units: **= 2 m^3**

Q1. State the equation that links density, mass and volume.

....

Q2. State the units of density, mass and volume.

....

Q3. Water has a density of 1000 kg/m^3 and oil has a density of 800 kg/m^3. State and explain whether the oil will float or sink in the water.

....

....

Q4. A book has a mass of 1 kg and a volume of 0.002 m^3. Calculate the density of the book.

Density = Mass ÷ Volume
= 1 kg ÷ 0.002 m^3
= _____ kg/m^3

Q5. A gold bar has a mass of 3.8 kg and a volume of 0.0002 m^3. Calculate the density of the gold bar.

Density = _____ ÷ _____
= _____ kg ÷ _____ m^3
= _____ kg/m^3

Q6. A rock has a mass of 300 kg and a volume of 0.1 m^3. Calculate the density of the rock.

Density = _____ ÷ _____
= _____ __ ÷ _____ __
= _____ ___

Q7. Steel has a density of 7800 kg/m^3. Calculate the volume of steel that has a mass of 3900 kg.

....

....

Q8. The average human body has a density of 995 kg/m^3.

a) Explain why humans can float on water.

....

b) Calculate the volume of a human body that has a mass of 70 kg.

....

....

Q9. A crate has a mass of 250 kg and a density of 50 kg/m^3. Calculate the volume of the crate.

....

....

Q10. A car has an average density of 280 kg/m^3 and a volume of 4.2 m^3. Calculate the mass of the car.

....

....

The atom

We have already learnt about the **particle model**, where matter is made of particles. This is one example of a **scientific model**.

Scientific models are usually simplified versions of an object or a phenomenon. This makes them easier to understand, while still representing the key features.

The particle model is used to explain and predict the behaviour of solids, liquids and gases. This is a simplification, as we know that particles are made of atoms and molecules (which, in turn, consist of smaller parts).

Models are also changed and updated over time, and the atomic model is one example of this. Previously, it was thought that atoms were indivisible (could not be broken down into anything smaller). This is the **Dalton model** of the atom.

However, newer evidence from experiments suggested the atom was made up of **sub-atomic particles**. They are called sub-atomic because they are smaller than the atom itself.

In the current model of the atom, there are three subatomic particles:

1. **Protons**. These have a positive charge and are contained in the centre of atom. The centre of the atom is called the **nucleus**.
2. **Neutrons** are also contained in the nucleus, but neutrons are neutral. Something that is neutral has no charge.
3. **Electrons** orbit around the nucleus. They have a negative charge.

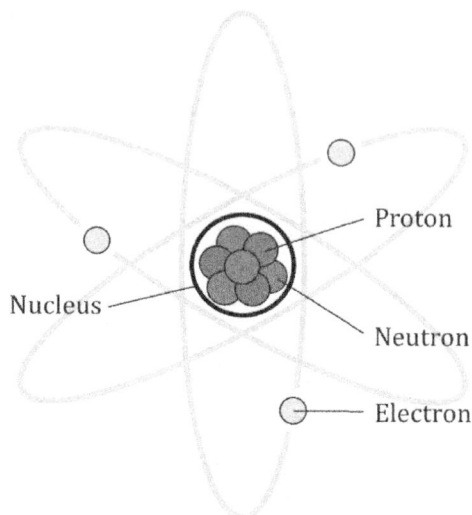

AG Caesar, CC BY-SA 4.0
<https://creativecommons.org/licenses/by-sa/4.0>, via Wikimedia Commons

Most of the mass of an atom is contained in the nucleus, with neutrons and protons having around 2000 times more mass than an electron.

Overall an atom is **neutral** as there are equal numbers of electrons and protons.

Generally, evidence is required to change a scientific model. New evidence and research go through a process called **peer review**.

Peer review is when other scientists look at the new evidence and decide whether or not it is valid. This is important as otherwise incorrect models and theories could be spread. After peer review, new research can be published. After this, other scientists may decide to try and **reproduce** the research to check whether the results are **repeatable**.

Q1. Describe the Dalton model of the atom.

....

....

Q2. The following questions are asking about the current model of the atom.

    a)   Describe where the nucleus of an atom is.

....

    b) Name the two sub-atomic particles that are in the nucleus.

....

    c) Name the sub-atomic particle that orbits around the nucleus.

....

    d) State the charge on a proton.

....

    e) State the charge on an electron.

....

    f) State the charge on a neutron.

....

    g) Name the sub-atomic particle that has the least mass.

....

Q3. Describe what a scientific model is.

....

....

Q4. Describe an advantage of using scientific models.

....

....

Q5. Describe what peer review is.

....

....

Q6. Describe the difference between the Dalton model and the current model of the atom.

....

....

Space

Mass and weight

Weight is a downwards force due to **gravity**. All objects have a force that attracts them towards each other. This force is due to gravity. Even you attract other objects to you because of gravity, but you have too little mass for the force to be very strong.

The **gravitational field strength (g)** at the surface of a planet is determined by its mass. The gravitational field strength on the surface of the Earth is **9.8 N/kg**.

The weight of an object can be calculated using the equation:

Weight = Mass x Gravitational field strength

The **mass** of an object is the amount of matter it contains and is measured in kilograms (kg). The mass of an object **stays the same** wherever it is, but its **weight can change** depending on the gravitational field strength.

Example question 1:

The moon has a gravitational field strength of 1.6 N/kg. Calculate the **weight** of a 20 kg mass on the surface of the moon.

Step 1. Write down equation: **Weight = Mass x Gravitational field strength**

Step 2. Insert variables into equation: **= 20 kg × 1.6 N/kg**

Step 3. Calculate answer. Remember units: **= 32 N**

We can also be asked questions to calculate mass or gravitational field strength. To answer these, we need to rearrange the equation.

Example question 2:

The gravitational field strength on Mars is 3.7 N/kg. An object on the surface of Mars has a weight of 0.74 N. Calculate the mass of the object

Step 1. Write down equation: **Weight = Mass x Gravitational field strength**

Step 2. Insert variables into equation: **0.74 N = Mass x 3.7 N/kg**

Step 3. Rearrange equation: **Mass = 0.74 N ÷ 3.7 N/kg**

Step 3. Calculate answer. Remember units: **= 0.2 kg**

Q1. State the equation that links weight, mass and gravitational field strength.

....

Q2. The following statements are either true or false. State which are true and which are false.

a) The mass of an object is the same everywhere.

....

b) The weight of an object is the same everywhere.

....

Q3. A book of mass 0.5 kg is on the surface of Earth. Calculate the weight of the book (the gravitational field strength on Earth is 9.8 N/kg).

Weight = Mass × Gravitational field strength

= 0.5 kg × 9.8 N/kg

= _____ N

Q4. The Lunar Rover vehicle had a mass of 210 kg. The gravitational field strength on the surface of the Moon is 1.6 N/kg. Calculate the weight of the Lunar Rover Vehicle.

Weight = Mass × Gravitational field strength

= _____ __ × ___ __

= _____ N

Q5. A rock of mass 2 kg is on the surface of Venus. The gravitational field strength on the surface of Venus is 8.8 N/kg. Calculate the weight of the rock.

Weight = Mass × Gravitational field strength

= _____ __ × ___ __

= _____ __

Q6. Pluto has a gravitational field strength of 0.5 N/kg. Calculate the weight of an object of mass 4 kg on the surface of pluto.

....

Q7. An object is on the surface of Ceres. The object has a weight of 0.81 N and a mass of 3 kg. Calculate the gravitational field strength on Ceres.

....

Q8. Dr Edmunds is leading a class expedition to Mercury. Dr Edmunds has a mass of 70 kg and a weight of 259 N. Calculate the gravitational field strength on Mercury.

....

Q9. The gravitational field strength at the top of Mount Everest is slightly less than at sea level, and is equal to 9.77 N/kg. Calculate the mass of a water bottle of weight 12 N.

....

Q10. A can of cola has a mass of 330 g and a weight of 2.3 N. Calculate the gravitational field strength.

....

Day, night and seasons

The Earth orbits around the Sun due to **gravity**.

The Earth also spins around an imaginary line called an **axis**. It completes one revolution every 24 hours.

24 hours is the length of a day, and it is this spinning of the Earth around its axis that causes day and night.

When one side of the Earth is facing towards the Sun, it is day-time.

When one side of the Earth is facing away from the Sun, it is night-time.

It takes the Earth 365 days to orbit around the Sun. This is the length of one **year**.

The axis of the earth is tilted 23.5° from vertical. This tilt, combined with the orbit around the Sun, causes the **seasons**.

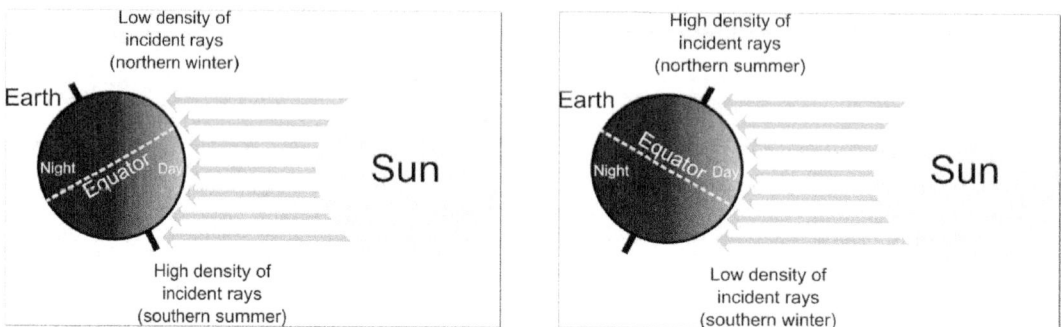

By Rhcastilhos - Own work, Public Domain, https://commons.wikimedia.org/w/index.php?curid=1577426

An imaginary line called the **equator** divides the Earth into two halves, called **hemispheres**.

When the northern hemisphere is tilted away from the Sun, it experiences a winter. This is because there is a lower intensity of light in the northern hemisphere.

When the northern hemisphere is tilted towards the Sun, it experiences a summer. This is because there is a higher intensity of light in the northern hemisphere.

When it is summer in the northern hemisphere, it is winter in the southern hemisphere (and vice versa).

During the summer, there are long days and short nights. During the winter, there are short days and long nights.

The Sun and other stars appear to move slowly in the sky. This is because the Earth is rotating. On Earth, the Sun appears to rise in the East and sets in the West.

Q1. Describe why the Earth orbits around the Sun.

....

Q2. State the name of the imaginary line the earth spins around.

....

Q3. State the length of a day in hours.

....

Q4. Describe what causes day and night on Earth

....

....

Q5. State how long it takes for the Earth to orbit around the Sun.

....

Q6. State what a hemisphere of the Earth is.

....

Q7. Describe when the northern hemisphere experiences a summer.

....

....

Q8. Describe when the southern hemisphere experiences a winter.

....

....

Q9. Describe how the length of the day compares to the length of the night in winter.

....

....

Q10. Describe why the Sun and other stars appear to move slowly in the sky.

....

....

Q11. State the direction the Sun appears to rise.

....

Q12. State the direction the Sun appears to set.

....

The solar system

The **solar system** consists of a star (the Sun) and eight **planets**. The Sun contains most of the mass of the solar system. Therefore, **gravitational forces** keep the planets in **orbit** around the Sun. The surface temperature of the Sun is around 6000°C, but this temperature is much greater below the Sun's surface.

There are eight **planets** that orbit around the Sun. In order from closest to furthest from the Sun, they are:

1. **Mercury**. The smallest planet and the one closest to the Sun.
2. **Venus**. There is a carbon dioxide atmosphere on Venus. Carbon dioxide is a greenhouse gas and so Venus is the hottest planet in the solar system.
3. **Earth**. Our own planet and the only known planet that has life.
4. **Mars**. Much colder than the Earth as it is further away from the Sun.
5. **Jupiter**. The largest planet in the solar system. Due to this, it has the largest gravitational field strength (equal to 25 N/kg). It is famous for its Great Red Spot which is a storm that has lasted for over 400 years.
6. **Saturn**. The second largest planet and has rings that are made of ice and rock.
7. **Uranus**. The third largest planet and rotates on its side.
8. **Neptune**. The furthest planet from the Sun and, because of this, has the lowest average temperature.

You might also have heard of **Pluto**. Pluto is a **dwarf planet** and is further away from the Sun than Neptune.

There is a mnemonic that can help you to remember the order of the planets: <u>M</u>y <u>V</u>ery <u>E</u>asy <u>M</u>ethod <u>J</u>ust <u>S</u>peeds <u>U</u>p <u>N</u>aming (<u>P</u>lanets).

WP, CC BY-SA 3.0 <https://creativecommons.org/licenses/by-sa/3.0>, via Wikimedia Commons

The four planets closest to the Sun are called the **terrestrial** (rocky) planets. Jupiter and Saturn are **gas giants**, while Uranus and Neptune are **ice giants**. Generally, the temperature of the planets decrease with distance from the Sun. The exception to this is Venus because of its carbon dioxide atmosphere.

Q1. State how many planets there are in the solar system.

....

Q2. Name the four terrestrial planets.

....

Q3. Name the two gas giants.

....

Q4. Name the two ice giants.

....

Q5. List the planets in the solar system, from nearest to the Sun to furthest from the Sun.

....

....

Q6. Name the planet that has the highest temperature. Explain why it has the highest temperature.

....

....

Q7. Name the object that contains most of the mass in the solar system.

....

Q8. State the force that keeps planets in orbit around the Sun.

....

Q9. Name the planet that has the lowest average surface temperature. Explain why it has the lowest temperature.

....

....

Q10. Name a dwarf planet in the solar system.

....

Q11. State the surface temperature of the Sun.

....

Q12. State the name of the planet that is the second largest in the solar system and has rings made of rock and ice.

....

Q13. Name the planet which has the largest gravitational field strength.

....

Beyond the solar system

The **universe** contains billions of different galaxies. A galaxy contains billions of stars. Our solar system is part of the **Milky Way galaxy**.

The image to the right shows an **artist's** impression of the Milky Way. We can also capture photographs of parts of it in the night sky.

The universe was formed 13.8 billion years ago in the **Big Bang**. We know this by looking at the light emitted by distant galaxies.

We measure the distance to distance galaxies in **light years**.

The speed of light is 300 000 000 m/s. A light year is the distance travelled by light in a time of one year. This is equal to 9.5×10^{15} m.

National Aeronautics and Space Administration, Public domain, via Wikimedia Commons

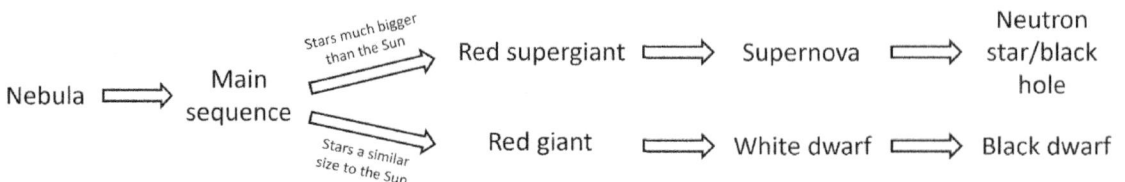

One example of a nearby (in astronomical terms) galaxy is the Andromeda galaxy. The Andromeda galaxy is 2.5 million light years away.

At the centre of the Milky Way galaxy is a **black hole**. A black hole is formed from the death of a very massive star.

Indeed, all stars go through a life cycle. All stars start off as a cloud of dust and gas (mostly hydrogen). This cloud of dust and gas is called a **nebula**. Gravitational attraction pulls this dust and gas together and eventually there is such a large amount of pressure and friction the temperature increases a lot. A **main sequence** star is formed.

When stars run out of hydrogen, they expand. Stars a similar size to our Sun form **red giants** and stars much bigger than our Sun form **red supergiants**.

Red giants leave behind a hot and small **white dwarf** which then cools to form a **black dwarf**. Red supergiants explode dramatically in a **supernova**. The biggest stars then leave behind a **black hole**, while less large stars leave behind a **neutron star**.

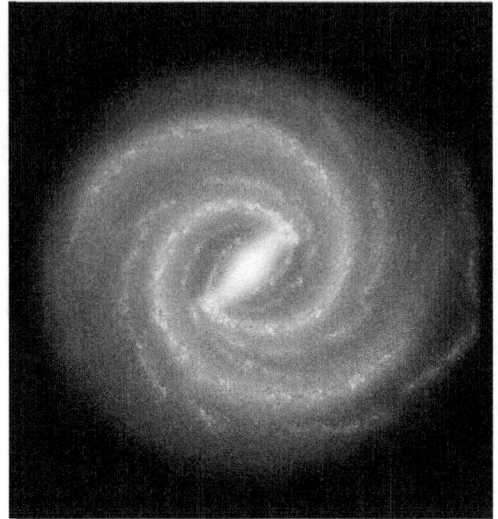

Nebula ⟹ Main sequence

Stars much bigger than the Sun ⟹ Red supergiant ⟹ Supernova ⟹ Neutron star/black hole

Stars a similar size to the Sun ⟹ Red giant ⟹ White dwarf ⟹ Black dwarf

Q1. The following statements are either true or false. State which are true and which are false.

a) A galaxy contains around 1000 stars.

....

b) The universe contains billions of galaxies.

....

c) A galaxy is bigger than the universe.

....

d) The universe was formed around 5000 years ago.

....

e) The speed of light is 300 000 000 m/s.

....

Q2. State the name of the galaxy that our solar system is in.

....

Q3. A light year is equal to 9.5×10^{15} m. The nearest star to Earth (other than the Sun) is Proxima Centauri. Proxima Centauri is 4.2 light years away, calculate this distance in metres.

....

....

Q4. State what is in the centre of our galaxy.

....

Q5. Describe what a nebula is.

....

Q6. Describe how a main sequence star is formed from a nebula.

....

....

Q7. A main sequence star runs out of hydrogen and forms a red giant. State the next two stages in the life cycle of this star.

....

Q8. State the name of an explosion of a red supergiant.

....

Q9. Describe when black holes are formed, and when neutron stars are formed.

....

....

Answers

Energy stores (page 7)
Q1. Gravitational potential
Q2. Kinetic
Q3. Thermal
Q4. Chemical
Q5. Their gravitational potential energy store decreases.
Q6. Their kinetic energy store increases.
Q7. The elastic potential energy store increases.
Q8. Chemical
Q9. Kinetic
Q10. Thermal
Q11. Electrostatic potential
Q12. Nuclear
Q13. Chemical
Q14. Magnetic potential

Energy transfers (page 9)
Q1. Energy is never created or destroyed; it is only transferred from one energy store to another.
Q2. Work done is another way of saying that energy is transferred from one store to another.
Q3. Joules
Q4. 30 J
Q5. Energy is wasted by raising the thermal energy store of the surroundings.
Q6. Mechanical, electrical, heating and by radiation.
Q7. EPE after firing = 0 J.
At maximum height: KE = 5 J, Total = 20 J.
Just before arrow hits ground: EPE = 0 J, KE = 20 J, Total = 20 J.

Power (page 11)
Q1. Power = Energy ÷ Time
Q2. Watts
Q3. 60 W
Q4. 20 W

Q5. 13 500 J
Q6. 180 000 J
Q7. 1000
Q8. 5000 W, 1500 W, 2 kW, 0.8 kW, 200 W
Q9. 2 640 000 J

Energy resources (page 13)
Q1. A non renewable resource is one which cannot be replaced once it has been used.
Q2. Oil, coal and gas.
Q3. A renewable resource is one that will not run out.
Q4. Wind, hydro-electric and solar
Q5. a) False b) True c) False
Q6. Burning fossil fuels releases carbon dioxide. Carbon dioxide is a greenhouse gas and so contributes to global warming.
Q7. Transport and heating.
Q8. There are no carbon dioxide emissions, so they don't contribute to global warming. Once built, there are no fuel costs and so are cheap to run.
Q9. The gravitational potential energy store is transferred into the kinetic energy store.
Q10. Coal and gas. Sulfur dioxide emissions lead to acid rain.
Q11. Burning fossil fuels produces a reliable output.

Electricity bills (page 15)
Q1. 1000
Q2. 3600
Q3. 3 600 000
Q4. 2.2 kWh
Q5. 1.6 kWh
Q6. 0.9 kWh
Q7. Total cost = energy transferred × price per kWh
Q8. £91.50
Q9. £76.75
Q10. £142.80

Thermal energy transfer (page 17)

Q1. Conduction, convection and radiation.

Q2. a) True b) True c) False d) False e) False f) True

Q3. Gases are very good insulators as their particles are very far apart from each other.

Q4. As a liquid or gas is heated, the particles move faster and become more spread out. Due to this they become less dense and therefore rise. Colder liquids or gases are more dense and sink.

Q5. As particles are heated, they vibrate more. These vibrations lead to collisions between particles and the vibrations are transferred onwards.

Q6. Black

Q7. There are no particles in a vacuum.

Q8. A conductor is a material that is able to conduct heat well.

Q9. Radiation

Reducing unwanted thermal energy transfers (page 19)

Q1. a) Cavity wall insulation b) loft insulation c) draught excluder

Q2. Reducing thermal energy losses reduces the amount of energy/fuel needed and so reduces the heating costs.

Q3. Gases are very good insulators, as their particles are so far apart from each other.

Q4. Closing the curtains.

Q5. Silvered surfaces reflect infrared radiation back into the food.

Q6. The shiny silver bottle reflects thermal energy away from the cold liquid and so would keep the liquid cooler for longer.

Q7. a) True b) True

Q8. The air inside the foam is a gas. Gases are very good insulators, as their particles are so far apart from each other.

Introduction to forces (page 23)

Q1. A Newton meter.

Q2. The Newton.

Q3. a) The forces are unbalanced b) 200 N to the left.

Q4. a) The forces are unbalanced b) 1000 N to the right c) It will accelerate to the right.

Q5. a) The forces are balanced. b) 0 N c) The aeroplane will continue at the same speed.

Q6. a) The forces are unbalanced b) 2000 N to the left. c) It will accelerate to the left (decelerate).

Types of force (page 25)

Q1. a) False b) False c) False d) True

Q2. A contact force is one that acts when two objects are physically touching each other.

Q3. Air resistance, friction, normal reaction, tension, thrust or upthrust.

Q4. A non-contact force acts between objects that are not touching each other.

Q5. Gravitational, magnetic or weight.

Q6. Upwards force labelled as air resistance. Downwards force labelled as weight.

Q7. a) If all individual forces make a resultant force of zero, we say the forces balanced.
b) The speed of the skydiver will remain constant.

Q8.

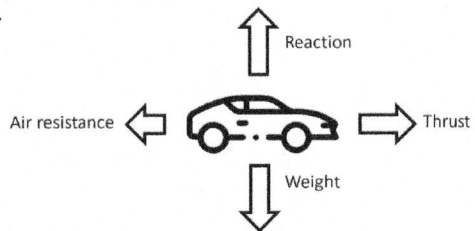

Q9. The car will accelerate forwards.

Hooke's law (page 27)

Q1. Newtons

Q2. Newtons per metre (N/m)

Q3. Metres

Q4. The extension of a spring is directly proportional to the force applied to it.

Q5. 0.4 N
Q6. 2 N
Q7. 1 N
Q8. Spring Y
Q9. 0.25 m
Q10. 8 N
Q11. 0.02 m

Moments (page 29)

Q1. Moment = Force × Perpendicular distance to pivot.

Q2. Distance is measured in metres. Force is measured in Newtons. Moments are measured Newton metres (Nm).

Q3. An object is balanced when the sum of the clockwise moments about a point are equal to the sum of the anticlockwise moments about the point.

Q4. a) 2 Nm b) 1.6 Nm c) 6 Nm

Q5. Not balanced (clockwise moment is 7.2 Nm, anticlockwise moment is 4 Nm).

Q6. Balanced (clockwise moment is 3.5 Nm, anticlockwise moment is also 3.5 Nm).

Pressure (page 31)

Q1. Pressure = Force ÷ Area

Q2. Pressure is measured in Pascals. Force is measured in Newtons. Area is measured in metres squared (m^2).

Q3. Atmospheric pressure decreases as we increase in height above Earth's surface. This is because as we go further from the Earth's surface there's less weight of air above us.

Q4. The lower hole in the bottle has the more weight of water above it and experiences the larger pressure. Water is pushed out of the lower hole at a higher speed.

Q5. 1300 Pa
Q6. 1000 Pa
Q7. 1250 Pa
Q8. 17 500 Pa

Q9. The high heel shoe will sink into the ground more as it has a smaller area and so would exert a higher pressure on the ground.

Speed (page 33)

Q1. Speed is a measure of how far an object has moved in a certain time.
Q2. 20 m
Q3. 8 m
Q4. 30 m/s
Q5. Speed = Distance ÷ Time
Q6. 6 m/s
Q7. 3 m/s
Q8. 1.2 m/s
Q9. 343 m/s
Q10. 300 000 000 m/s
Q11. 10 000 m
Q12. 800 m

Distance-time graphs (page 35)

Q1. The speed of an object.
Q2. Speed = distance ÷ time
Q3. a) 5 m/s b) 1.5 m/s c) 2 m/s d) 1 m/s e) 12.5 m/s f) 9 m/s

Terminal velocity (page 37)

Q1. The air resistance increases.
Q2. The speed of the car remains constant at 70 mph.
Q3. The car accelerates forwards.
Q4. Weight is larger than air resistance so there is a resultant force downwards. The skydiver will be accelerating.
Q5. The forces are balanced as weight and air resistance are equal in size. The skydiver will be falling at a constant speed.
Q6. The air resistance is larger than the weight so there is a resultant force upwards. The skydiver will be decelerating.
Q7. When the skydiver reaches a certain speed, the air resistance is equal to the weight. Therefore, there is no resultant force. Due to Newton's first law, the speed of the skydiver remains the same.

Q8. When the skydiver opens their parachute, they have a much larger surface area. This increases the air resistance and there is a resultant force upwards. This means the skydiver decelerates.

Q9.

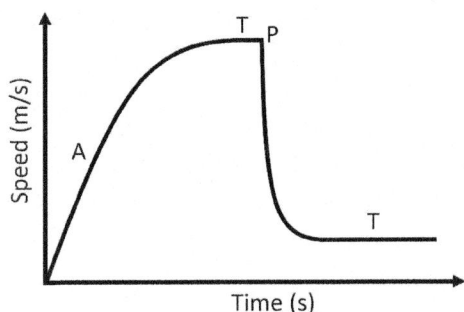

Introduction to waves (page 41)
Q1. a) True b) False c) True d) True e) False
Q2.

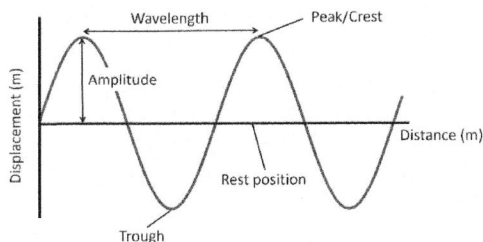

Q3. In a longitudinal wave, a rarefaction is where the particles are furthest apart.
Q4. Both longitudinal and transverse waves are caused by vibrations. They both also transfer energy from one place to another.
Q5. Transverse waves are caused by a vibration that is perpendicular to the direction of wave travel. Longitudinal waves are caused by a vibration that is parallel to the direction of wave travel.
Sound (page 43)
Q1. An object that is vibrating makes a sound wave.
Q2. A longitudinal wave is caused by vibrations that are parallel to the direction of wave travel.
Q3. Frequency is a measure of how many sound waves pass a point every second.
Q4. 20 000

Q5. Compressions are formed when particles are closest together. Rarefactions are formed the particles are furthest apart.
Q6. a) False b) False c) True d) True
Q7.

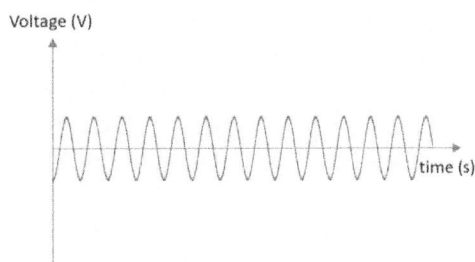

Speed of sound (page 45)
Q1. a) False b) True c) False
Q2. 250 m/s
Q3. Human reaction time would mean the measured time would be too long. The equation for speed is speed = total distance divided by time and so if the time is longer, the speed would be less (as you're dividing the same distance by a larger number).
Q4. Distance = speed × time
Q5. 85 m
Q6. 136 m
Water waves and superposition (page 47)
Q1. a) False b) False c) True d) True
Q2. Water waves (or any electromagnetic wave).
Q3. Transverse waves are formed by a vibration that is perpendicular to the direction of wave travel.
Q4. The two waves superpose to give a wave with a larger amplitude (and the same frequency).

Q5. The two waves superpose and cancel each other out to give a flat line with no amplitude.

Q6. The two waves superpose and partially cancel each other out. This creates a wave with a lower amplitude than that of the first wave.

Reflection (page 49)

Q1. a) True b) True c) False d) False e) False f) False

Q2. 300 000 000 m/s

Q3. The angle of incidence is equal to the angle of reflection.

Q4. Specular reflections happen when rays of light are reflected from a very smooth surface like a mirror. If rays of light are shone onto a surface that isn't smooth then a diffuse reflection happens. Here, rays are reflected at many angles.

Q5.

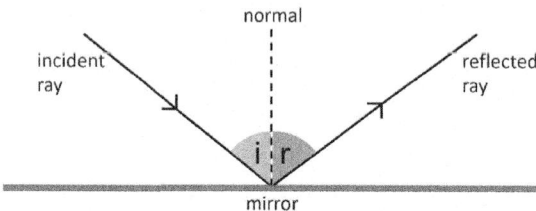

Refraction (page 51)

Q1. a) False b) True c) True d) True

Q2.

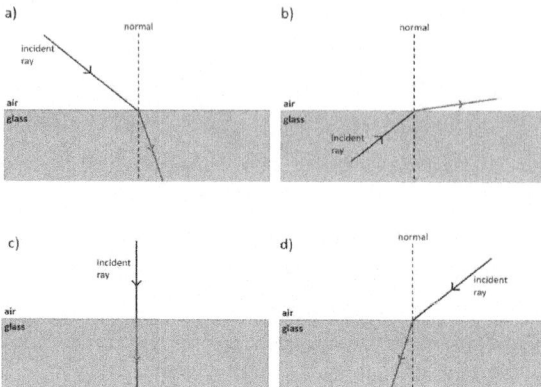

Q3. The illusion happens because of refraction. Light rays are reflected from all parts of the pencil. If light is coming from part of the pencil that is under the water, then it is refracted away from the normal. If light is coming from part of the pencil that is over the water, then there is no refraction. This makes the pencil look bent.

The human eye (page 53)

Q1. a) True b) True c) False d) True

Q2. In glasses, magnifying glasses and telescopes.

Q3.

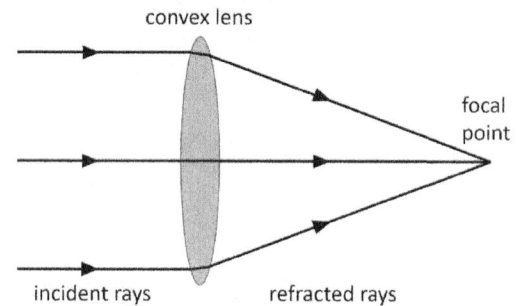

Q4. A convex lens is wider in the middle that it is at the edges. Because of this, rays of light refract by different amounts depending on where they hit the lens.

Q5. When it is very bright, the iris will be mostly closed to protect the retina from damage. When it is dark, the iris will be more open to allow more light to reach the retina.

Q6. Lens b) is more curved than lens a). It therefore refracts light by a larger amount and has a focal point closer to the lens.

Cameras (page 55)

Q1. A translucent material is one that allows for some light to pass through it.

Q2. An inverted image is one that is upside down.

Q3. a) True b) True c) False d) False

Q4. Refraction is when light changes direction when it travels from one material to another. A convex lens is wider in the middle that it is at the edges. Because of this, rays of light refract by different amounts depending on where they hit the lens.

Q5.

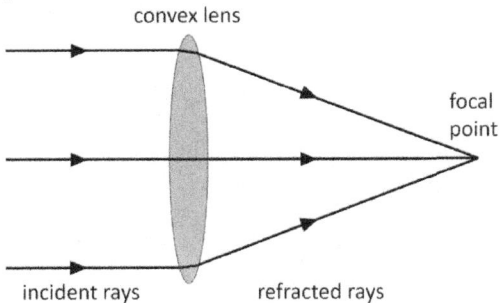

Colours in light (page 57)

Q1. a) False b) True c) True d) False e) True

Q2. Dispersion happens because the different colours of light experience a different refractive index and so refract by different amounts.

Q3. Red, orange, yellow, green, blue, indigo, violet.

Q4. Orange.

Q5. A blue object looks blue because it reflects blue light into our eyes.

Q6. a) Yellow

b) A blue object only reflects blue light. As yellow light is shone onto the blue object, it will reflect no light and appear black.

Introduction to static electricity (page 61)

Q1. Protons and neutrons.

Q2. The electron. Electrons have a negative charge.

Q3. Non-contact. Object do not need to touch for a non-contact force to act.

Q4. An ion.

Q5. Atoms are neutral as they have equal number of protons and electrons.

Q6. Objects gain a static charge when one object rubs against another.

Q7. a) True b) False c) False

Q8. If somebody rubs a balloon against their hair, the friction transfers electrons from their hair onto the balloon. If the balloon is removed from their hair, then the balloon will attract the hair. This is because the balloon and the hair have opposite charges.

Q9. Friction between the person's feet and the carpet will mean that electrons will be transferred and a static charge will build up. This charge will be discharged if the person touches a metal door handle as metal is a conductor.

Electric field lines (page 63)

Q1. Electric field lines point away from a positive charge and towards a negative charge.

Q2. A contact force is one that acts when two objects are physically touching each other. A non-contact force acts between objects that are not touching each other.

Q3. Non-contact

Q4. Repel

Q5.

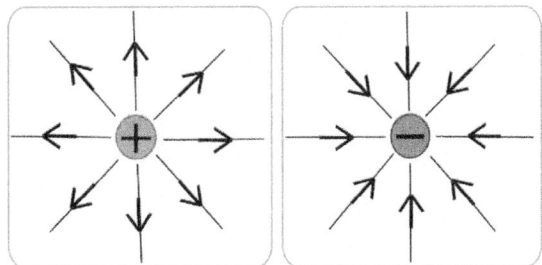

Q6. The electric field lines represent the direction of force that a nearby positive charge would experience.

Q7. The further you go from a charge, the weaker the field becomes.

Q8.

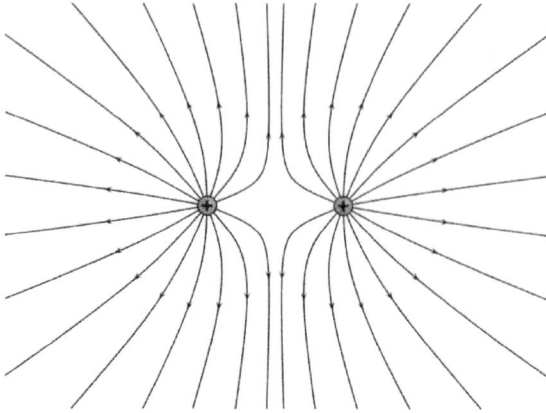

Geek3, CC BY-SA 4.0 <https://creativecommons.org/licenses/by-sa/4.0>, via Wikimedia Commons

Circuit symbols (page 65)

Q1. An ammeter measures the current in a circuit.

Q2. There's only one path for current to flow in a series circuit. There's more than one path for the current to flow in a parallel circuit.

Q3. A battery is made of more than one cell.

Q4. a) False b) False

Q5.

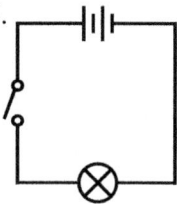

Q6.

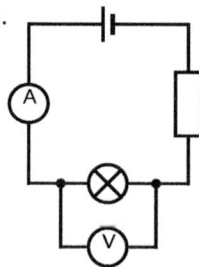

Q7.

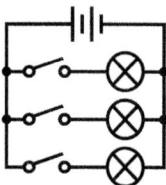

Current (page 67)

Q1. a) True b) False c) False d) False

Q2. An ammeter.

Q3. Amps

Q4.

cell   lamp   ammeter

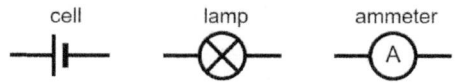

Q5.

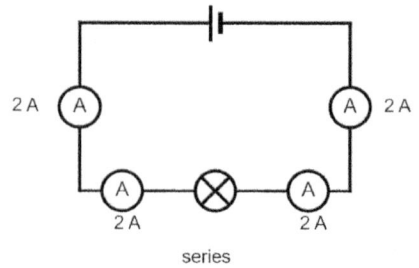

2 A   2 A

2 A   2 A

series

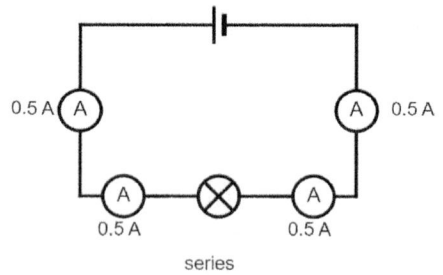

0.5 A   0.5 A

0.5 A   0.5 A

series

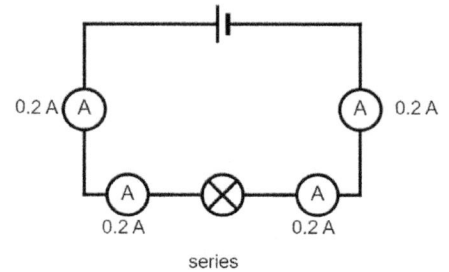

0.2 A   0.2 A

0.2 A   0.2 A

series

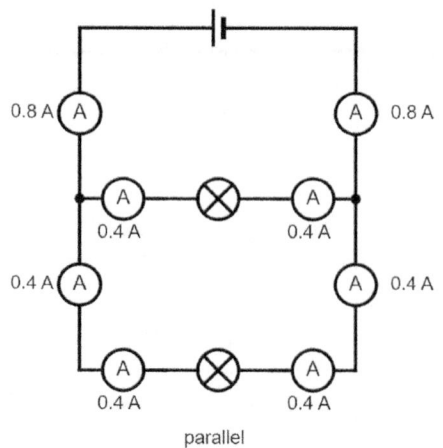

0.8 A   0.8 A

0.4 A   0.4 A

0.4 A   0.4 A

0.4 A   0.4 A

parallel

Q5. (continued)

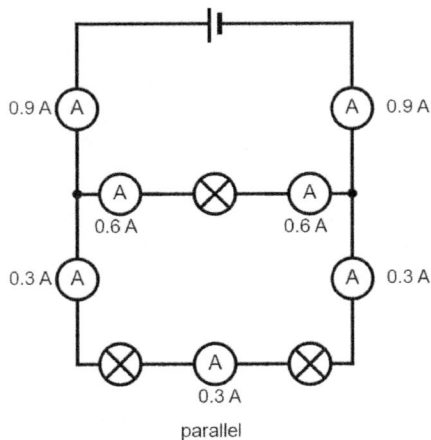

parallel

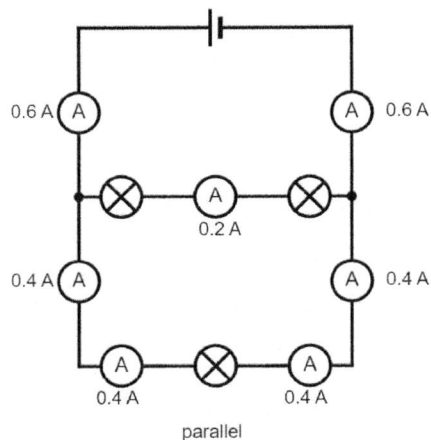

parallel

Q4.

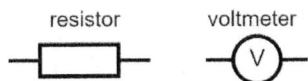

Potential difference (page 69)

Q1. a) True b) False c) True d) False e) False

Q2. Each lamp receives the full potential difference and so is brighter. Each lamp can also be turned on and off independently.

Q3.

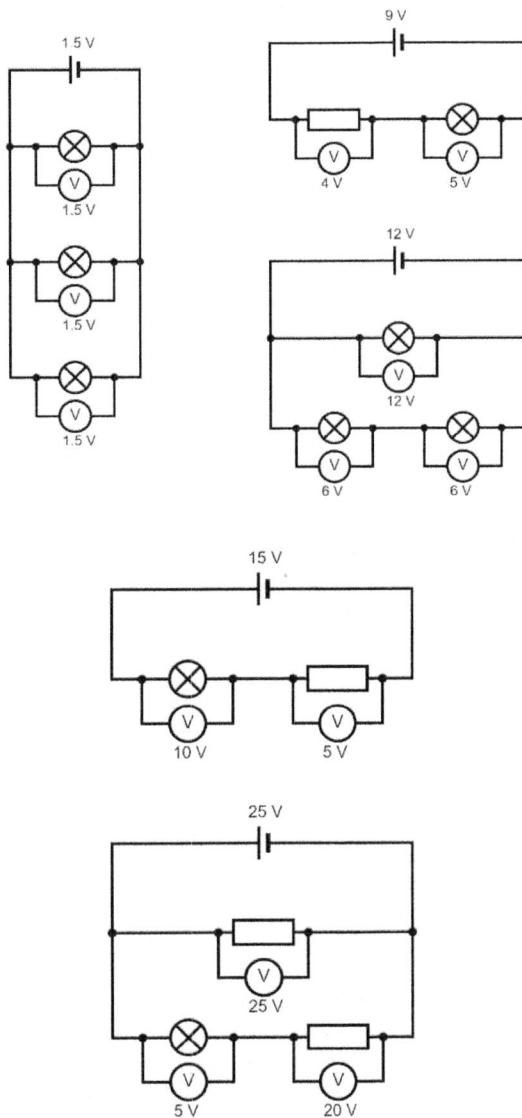

resistor   voltmeter

Resistance (page 71)

Q1. V = I × R

Q2. Ohms (Ω)

Q3. Electrical conductors have a low resistance, while insulators have a high resistance.

Q4. 30 V

Q5. 50 V

Q6. 60 Ω

Q7. 80 V

Q8. 300 Ω

Q9. 750 V

Q10. 0.005 A

Introduction to magnetism (page 73)

Q1. Magnetic field lines point away from the North pole and towards the South pole.

Q2. A contact force is one that acts when two objects are touching each other. A non-contact force acts between objects that are not touching each other.

Q3. Non-contact

Q4.

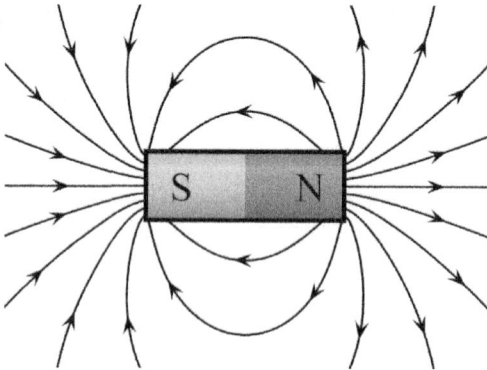

Q5. Iron, nickel and cobalt.

Q6. a) True b) True c) False d) True e) True f) False g) False

Plotting magnetic fields (page 75)

Q1. a) False b) True c) True

Q2. A plotting compass is a small bar magnet that is free to rotate.

Q3. Molten iron and nickel.

Q4. Cobalt.

Q5. Compasses also show the direction of the magnetic field.

Q6. The field caused by the electronic device would deflect the compass.

Q7. Near the poles of the Earth because the magnetic field lines are closest together.

Q8. No, compasses point towards magnetic south so require a magnetic field to work.

Electromagnetism (page 77)

Q1. Current

Q2. A solenoid is a coil of wire.

Q3. Inside the solenoid.

Q4. By increasing the number of turns in the coil, by increasing the current, or by adding an iron core.

Q5. A soft magnetic material can be easily magnetised and de-magnetised. A hard magnetic material is difficult to magnetise and de-magnetise.

Q6. Iron

Q7. A hard magnetic material shouldn't be used in the core of a solenoid as it would retain some magnetism.

Q8. The magnetic field gets weaker.

Q9. The magnetic field around a current carrying wire is in concentric circles around the wire.

Q10. The current.

Q11. The direction of the magnetic field lines.

Q12. By using plotting compasses.

Electric motors (page 79)

Q1. a) True b) False

Q2. A coil of wire, a permanent magnet, a split ring commutator and carbon brushes.

Q3. The current creates a magnetic field. This magnetic field interacts with the permanent field that surrounds the coil. This interaction produces a force.

Q4. A split ring commutator reverses the direction of current every half turn. This ensures the motor continues to rotate in the same direction.

Q5. By increasing the current flowing through the coil, by increasing the number of turns in the coil or by increasing the strength of the magnetic field.

Q6. By either reversing the direction of current or by reversing the direction of the magnetic field.

Q7. Carbon

Q8. Without a current, there is no magnetic field and therefore no force.

Q9. As the current has decreased, the strength of the magnetic field reduces. This reduces the size of the force and therefore The motor will spin less quickly.

Speakers and microphones (page 81)

Q1. a) True b) True c) False d) True e) False

Q2. A coil of wire, a permanent magnet and a cone.

Q3. A current that is constantly changing direction is called an alternating current.

Q4. A current flows into the coil of wire. This makes a magnetic field, which then interacts with the permanent field. This creates a force on the cone (causing it to move). Because there is an alternating current, the direction of the force is constantly changing. This causes a vibration of the cone. This produces sound.

Q5. By increasing the current flowing through the coil, by increasing the number of turns in the coil or by increasing the strength of the magnetic field caused by the permanent magnet.

Q6. A sound wave comes onto the diaphragm and causes it to vibrate. This causes the coil of wire to vibrate and the coil moves within the magnetic field of the permanent magnet. This causes a current to flow in the coil.

Particle model (page 85)

Q1.

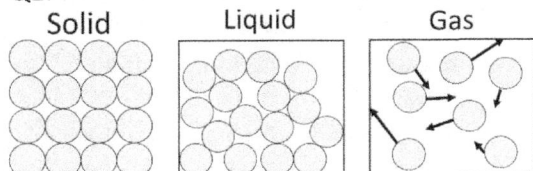

Q2. Gas

Q3. Liquid

Q4. Gas

Q5. Gas

Q6. Solid

Q7. Liquid

Q8. Liquid

Q9. The speed increases.

Q10. Gas particles move around quickly in random directions, at a range of speeds.

Q11. In a solid, particles are arranged in a regular pattern and vibrate around fixed positions. As a solid melts, the particles will be able to move and flow past each other. The particles are still held closely together, though.

Q12. In a liquid, particles are held closely together but are free to flow past each other. As the liquid turns into a gas, the particles will move away from each other and move quickly in random directions.

Q13. Ice is less dense than water.

State changes (page 87)

Q1. The mass before a state change is the same as the mass after a state change.

Q2. Melting

Q3. Condensation

Q4. Boiling or evaporation.

Q5. Deposition

Q6. Sublimation

Q7. Freezing

Q8. 0 °C

Q9. 100 °C

Q10. In a solid, particles are arranged in a regular pattern and vibrate around fixed positions.

Q11. In a gas, the particles are far apart from each other and they move around quickly in random directions.

Q12. a) False b) True c) False d) False

Q13. Solid as the temperature is less than the melting point of water.

Q14. Gas as the temperature is more than the boiling point of water.

Q15. Liquid as the temperature is between the melting and boiling points of water.

Heating and cooling curves (page 89)

Q1.

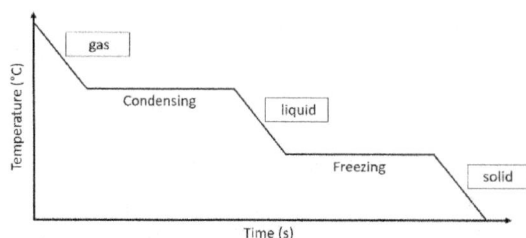

Q2. A pure substance is made from only one element or compound.

Q3. As gas particles cool, they move more slowly and their kinetic energy decreases.

Q4. Internal energy consists of the kinetic energy and potential energy stores of the particles.

Q5. An impure substance contains more than one element or compound.

Q6. For an impure substance, there is not a single temperature for melting and boiling. Instead, this happens over a range of temperatures.

Q7. While a solid is melting, energy goes into breaking the bonds (instead of increasing the temperature).

Q8. The internal energy increases.

Pressure in gases (page 91)

Q1. Brownian motion. This happens because of collisions with air particles that are moving in random directions and at a range of different speeds.

Q2. a) The number of air particles increases.

b) The number of collisions increases.

c) The force increases.

d) The pressure increases.

e) The size of the balloon increases.

Q3. a) The force increases.

b) The pressure increases.

Q4. The average speed of gas particles increases.

Q5. Container A has the higher pressure. The smaller volume means the particles will collide with the walls of the container more often.

Q6. Container B has the higher pressure. This is because the higher temperature means that particles in container B will be moving more quickly. This means more frequent collisions with the walls of the container, and therefore a higher pressure.

Q7. As the air inside the balloon cools, the particles will move more slowly. This means less frequent collisions with the walls of the balloon and therefore a lower pressure. The balloon will decrease in size.

Diffusion (page 93)

Q1. a) False b) False c) False d) True

Q2. In a liquid, particles are held closely together but are free to flow past each other.

Q3. In a gas, the particles are far apart from each other and they move around quickly in random directions.

Q4. Diffusion is the movement of particles from a high concentration (of those particles) to a lower concentration.

Q5. The average speed increases.

Q6. Diffusion will be fastest in beaker B. This is because particles move faster in a hotter liquid.

Q7. The deodorant would collide with the air particles in the room. The collisions would spread the deodorant particles out from a higher concentration to a lower concentration.

Q8. It would increase the rate of diffusion.

Density (page 95)

Q1. Density = mass ÷ volume

Q2. Density has units of kg/m^3, mass has units of kg and volume has units of m^3.

Q3. Oil will float on water as it has a lower density.

Q4. 500 kg/m^3

Q5. $19\,000 \text{ kg/m}^3$

Q6. 3000 kg/m^3

Q7. 0.5 m^3

Q8. a) Because humans have a lower density than water.

b) 0.07 m^3

Q9. 5 m^3

Q10. 1176 kg

The atom (page 97)

Q1. In the Dalton model, atoms were indivisible.

Q2. a) In the centre of the atom.

b) Protons and neutrons.

c) The electron.

d) Positive

e) Negative

f) No charge (neutral).

g) The electron.

Q3. A scientific model is a simplified version of an object or phenomenon.

Q4. They are easier to understand, while still representing the key features.

Q5. Peer review is when other scientists look at new evidence and decide whether or not it is valid.

Q6. In the Dalton model, atoms were indivisible. In the current model of the atom, there are three subatomic particles.

Mass and weight (page 101)

Q1. $W = m \times g$

Q2. a) True b) False

Q3. 4.9 N

Q4. 336 N

Q5. 17.6 N

Q6. 2 N

Q7. 0.27 N/kg

Q8. 3.7 N/kg

Q9. 1.23 kg

Q10. 6.97 N/kg

Day, night and seasons (page 103)

Q1. Due to gravity.

Q2. The axis.

Q3. 24 hours.

Q4. The spinning of Earth around its axis causes day and night.

Q5. 365 days (one year).

Q6. The Earth is divided into two halves (called hemispheres).

Q7. The northern hemisphere experiences a summer when it is tilted towards the Sun. This is because there would be a higher intensity of light in the northern hemisphere.

Q8. The southern hemisphere experiences a winter when it is tilted away from the Sun. This is because there would be a lower intensity of light in the southern hemisphere.

Q9. The length of the day is shorter than the night in the winter.

Q10. The Sun and other stars appear to move slowly in the sky because the Earth is rotating.

Q11. The Sun appears to rise in the East.

Q12. The Sun appears to set in the West.

The solar system (page 105)

Q1. There are eight planets in the Solar system.

Q2. Mercury, Venus, Earth and Mars.

Q3. Jupiter and Saturn.

Q4. Uranus and Neptune.

Q5. Mercury, Venus, Earth, Mars, Jupiter, Saturn, Uranus and Neptune.

Q6. Venus is the hottest planet as it has a carbon dioxide atmosphere. Carbon dioxide is a greenhouse gas.

Q7. The Sun.

Q8. Gravitational forces.

Q9. Neptune has the lowest average temperature as it is the furthest planet from the Sun.

Q10. Pluto
Q11. 6000 °C
Q12. Saturn
Q13. Jupiter
Beyond the solar system (page 107)
Q1. a) False b) True c) False d) False e) True
Q2. The Milky Way.
Q3. 3.99×10^{16} m
Q4. A black hole.
Q5. A nebula is a cloud of dust and gas.
Q6. Gravitational attraction pulls a nebula together and eventually there is such a large amount of pressure and friction that the temperature increases a lot. A main sequence star is then formed.
Q7. The red giant forms a white dwarf and then a black dwarf.
Q8. A supernova.
Q9. After a supernova, the biggest stars leave behind a black hole. Less large stars leave behind a neutron star.

Printed in Great Britain
by Amazon